NOLO *Your Legal Companion*

"In Nolo you can trust." —THE NEW YORK TIMES

Whether you have a simple question or a complex problem, turn to us at:

NOLO.COM

Your all-in-one legal resource

Need quick information about wills, patents, adoptions, starting a business—or anything else that's affected by the law? **Nolo.com** is packed with free articles, legal updates, resources and a complete catalog of our books and software.

NOLO NOW

Make your legal documents online

Creating a legal document has never been easier or more cost-effective! Featuring Nolo's Online Will, as well as online forms for LLC formation, incorporation, divorce, name change—and many more! Check it out at **http://nolonow.nolo.com**.

NOLO'S LAWYER DIRECTORY

Meet your new attorney

If you want advice from a qualified attorney, turn to Nolo's Lawyer Directory—the only directory that lets you see hundreds of in-depth attorney profiles so you can pick the one that's right for you. Find it at **http://lawyers.nolo.com**.

ALWAYS UP TO DATE

Sign up for NOLO'S LEGAL UPDATER

Old law is bad law. We'll email you when we publish an updated edition of this book—sign up for this free service at nolo.com/legalupdater.

Find the latest updates at NOLO.COM

Recognizing that the law can change even before you use this book, we post legal updates during the life of this edition at **nolo.com/updates**.

Is this edition the newest? ASK US!

To make sure that this is the most recent edition available, just give us a call

D0813845

Please note

We believe accurate, plain-English legal information should help you solve many of your own legal problems. But this text is not a substitute for personalized advice from a knowledgeable lawyer. If you want the help of a trained professional—and we'll always point out situations in which we think that's a good idea—consult an attorney licensed to practice in your state.

1st edition

Hiring Your
First Employee

A Step-by-Step Guide

by Fred S. Steingold

FIRST EDITION	MAY 2008
Editor	BARBARA KATE REPA
Cover & Book Design	SUSAN PUTNEY
Production	SARAH HINMAN
Proofreading	ANI DIMUSHEVA
Index	MEDEA MINNICH
Printing	DELTA PRINTING SOLUTIONS, INC.

Steingold, Fred.

Hiring your first employee : a step-by-step guide / by Fred S. Steingold. -- 1st ed.

p. cm.

ISBN-13: 978-1-4133-0859-4 (pbk.)

ISBN-10: 1-4133-0859-7 (pbk.)

1. Employee selection--Law and legislation--United States--Popular works. 2. Employees--Recruiting--Law and legislation--United States--Popular works. 3. Labor contract--United States--Popular works. 4. Labor laws and legislation--United States--Popular works. I. Title.

KF3457.Z9S74 2008

658.3'11--dc22

2007051624

Quantity sales: For information on bulk purchases or corporate premium sales, please contact the Special Sales Department. For academic sales or textbook adoptions, ask for Academic Sales. Call 800-955-4775 or write to Nolo, 950 Parker Street, Berkeley, CA 94710.

Acknowledgment

I wish to thank Barbara Kate Repa for her elegant editing—and her unflagging enthusiasm for this project.

Table of Contents

Deciding Whether to Hire an Employee

I f you're used to running your business lean or alone, you have lots of company. More than 20 million businesses—about 70% of all the businesses in the United States—have no employees. The great majority of these small businesses are owned by one person, or perhaps two or three, who handle the required tasks on their own—from filing the startup paperwork to dealing with daily details that keep the concern going. In addition to producing goods or services that are the lifeblood of the business, these entrepreneurs' days can be filled with a host of activities from the exciting to the mundane: reeling in prospective new customers or clients, writing marketing copy, ordering supplies, sweeping the front entryway.

Some business owners decide from the start that they can't do all the work themselves; they hire an employee as part of the start-up process. But most businesses start out without employees, running lean until they see how the enterprise develops. And many small business owners never hire anyone to help.

Some owners are content for their businesses to remain tiny—and for them, it makes little sense to hire an employee. If you think this might be your situation, this chapter will quickly help you decide whether it is best to stay employee-free.

But it's possible that you may not realize that having an employee can help your businesses grow—and make your life easier. Or you may simply be held back by a fear that hiring a worker is complicated and likely to create painful legal and accounting headaches. If so, you may be needlessly depriving yourself of the opportunity to reap higher profits from your business, and to establish a more efficient and fulfilling operation.

As you read this book, you'll soon learn that if your business could benefit by adding an employee, a fear of hiring is misguided. Anyone with the intelligence and gumption to create a business is perfectly capable of becoming an employer—and of doing so without the expensive help of lawyers, accountants, or human resource specialists.

If you're just starting a business and you've decided to hire an employee from the get-go, this book will lead you through the process so that you won't stumble along the way. If you're already in business and you—and any co-owners—are scraping by without any extra help, you'll learn how having employees can help your business thrive, and how to take the steps required to bring the first one on board. And finally, if you've already hired an employee but aren't sure whether you've followed all the necessary steps, this book will serve as a reassuring checklist, enabling you to spot and correct any missteps you may have taken.

When Hiring an Employee May Not Be Wise

Making the leap from entrepreneur to employer is not for everyone. You may have understandable and legitimate reasons not to hire an employee, or at least to hold off for the present. For example, you may:

- not know what the demand will be for the goods and services your new business will offer
- feel it's prudent not to expand too quickly
- be able to cover business overloads by working extra hours, or occasionally calling on family members to help
- not have the time, patience, or desire to train and supervise another person
- despise extra paperwork, even in small amounts
- be reluctant to reveal trade secrets or other sensitive information to a nonowner, or
- not have space for an employee.

The information in the book will help you analyze whether hiring an employee is a good step to take now or in the future. (See "Options Other Than Hiring an Employee," below.)

What an Employee Can Do for Business

If you own or co-own a small business, you're probably reading this book because you're considering hiring your first employee. When pondering whether to make the move, consider what an employee may be able to do to help you and your business.

Perform Routine Tasks

Many business owners find that adding an employee relieves them of the drudgery of doing mundane tasks, such as entering data or updating customer lists. Others relish help with more sophisticated duties, such as calling potential customers or billing clients. The key is to acknowledge that you enjoy and excel at some tasks more than others, and that having other people to help can free you to make the most productive and satisfying use of your own time and talents.

> EXAMPLE: Ann has been in the apartment rental business for five years, and now owns 35 units in eight different buildings. She is feeling worn down by having to do everything herself and would like to spend more time on what she likes to do best: finding additional properties and fixing up the units she owns so that she can get more rent from them. Ann hires an assistant to help with settling new tenants, collecting rent, and maintaining the properties.

Increase Business Hours

There's a limit to how much time you can personally devote to being on the job. Adding an employee can make it possible to increase business hours to serve customers at times when you can't, or would prefer not to be, on call.

> EXAMPLE: Tom has a kiosk in a shopping mall where he sells decorative craft items. Because he wants to spend time with his family, Tom has limited his hours to 48 hours a week. But he laments missing potential

business from shoppers who pass by when his kiosk is closed. Tom hires an employee to run the kiosk in the evenings and on Sundays.

Add New Skills

Your particular talents and skills determine—but may also limit—what you're able to offer to customers and clients. By hiring an employee, you may be able to complement your own skills, which may make it possible for you to offer a wider range of products and services to potential customers—or even change the nature of your business to make it more profitable.

EXAMPLE: Jaime and Betty, both of whom are accomplished copywriters, formed a small company offering copywriting services to high-tech businesses. They're doing well, but realize that they can attract even more clients if, in addition to imparting their finesse with words, they can promise visually appealing print and online products. They hire their first employee—a graphics designer who has experience in creating eye-catching written material.

Expand the Business

Once you become established, you may find yourself turning down lucrative new business because your time and resources are too tapped. Hiring an employee can increase your capacity—and your bottom line.

EXAMPLE: Rita provides daily janitorial services for a small office building. The building's owner is about to buy a second building nearby and would like to have Rita take over the janitorial responsibilities there as well. Rita would welcome some additional income, but knows she can't handle all the additional work by herself. The solution: She hires an employee whom she'll train and supervise, making it possible for her business to handle both properties.

Home-Based Businesses: Check on Zoning First

Local ordinances often divide cities and towns into zones such as residential, office, retail, and industrial. If you live in a residential zone and have a home-based business, be sure to check your community's zoning ordinance, which is available at your city or town hall or online. The ordinance may affect your decision to hire an employee.

While some ordinances are silent on the subject, others limit employees to family members or people living in the home, or only permit one or two employees who are nonresidents. And some completely prohibit adding an employee.

In addition to public zoning ordinances, you may also have to comply with private regulations concerning having a business in your home, especially if you live in a condominium or planned development. These private regulations may be found in Covenants, Conditions, and Restrictions (CC&Rs) that apply to your neighborhood or condo development. They may also appear in your deed or in a document called Building and Use Restrictions.

If you're a tenant rather than an owner, you should also check to see whether your lease contains any restrictions on having an employee.

When You Can't Do It All Yourself

There's no specific rule for when it's time to consider hiring your first employee. But there may be early indicators that you'd be wise to take the plunge and bring in another worker to help make your business operate more efficiently or lucratively.

Heed this warning, for example, if you increasingly:

- are too busy to take on work that you'd love to have
- get complaints from customers and clients about missing promised delivery dates
- feel the need to expand your business hours

- want to broaden the products or services your business provides
- yearn to rid yourself of some of the work that's drudgery so you can spend time on more pleasant and profitable activities, or
- lack time to take a vacation or attend to your own health or family matters.

Many of these concerns can be alleviated simply by hiring an employee to share the load.

Options Other Than Hiring an Employee

If you're feeling frazzled or you're losing out on possible profits because you lack needed help in running your business, you may be able to address the problem—at least partially—by taking steps other than hiring an employee.

Adding a Co-Owner

If you're the sole owner of the business, you can bring in another person as a partner to share the work and the business concerns. And if you already have a co-owner or two, you can invite another one to join you.

Disadvantages of adding a co-owner. The downside of having co-owners is that you'll have to share the profits, so that you and any current co-owners will each receive a smaller share of the pie. And the more owners you have, the greater the chances that you won't see eye-to-eye on some issues; management disputes can be draining.

Advantages of adding a co-owner. First and foremost, you don't have to worry about having enough money in the till to cover periodic paychecks. In fact, you'll likely have fewer cash worries in general, since a co-owner will usually bring an infusion of cash as the price of owning a piece of the business.

Also, you're not likely to get stuck with half-hearted help. A co-owner has a stake in how well the business does, and almost certainly will work harder than an employee would.

Leasing a Worker

Many employment agencies have a roster of experienced employees you can lease. Technically, a worker hired through such an agency won't be an employee of your business, but an employee of the agency.

In such arrangements, the agency handles all the necessary paperwork—including cutting the checks to pay the worker's wages and cover employment taxes. If the worker turns out to be a bad fit for your business, you're usually free to terminate the lease at any time, which can feel easier than firing an employee you have personally sought out and hired.

If the worker is a stellar match for your business, you'll probably be able to hire him or her after a time.

Disadvantages of leasing an employee. The employment agency makes money by charging for its efforts—which usually involve advertising for qualified workers, screening them, and handling paychecks for you—so it will tack on a hefty fee. You'll typically pay more for leasing help than if you hired a worker directly, though this might not be true if your alternative is to pay for a protracted search for the right employee.

Another possible drawback is that a leased worker is less likely to form bonds of loyalty with your business than an employee you search out and mentor.

Advantages of leasing an employee. By going through a leasing agency, you avoid the time, effort, and expense of a prolonged search for the right employee.

In addition, you don't have to deal with pay checks and employment taxes. And you can easily end the relationship if the leased employee is a dud.

Hiring an Independent Contractor

An independent contractor is someone who performs services for others but does not have the legal status of an employee. Most people who qualify as independent contractors have their own trade, business, or profession. They're in business for themselves.

The IRS prefers to have workers classified as employees because it believes that independent contractors are relatively unreliable when it comes to paying taxes. If you treat a worker as an independent contractor, and the IRS classifies that person as an employee, you'll be liable for employment taxes for the worker, and may also be charged a penalty for your erroneous actions.

Under IRS guidelines, whether a worker is an employee or an independent contractor depends largely on how much control you have over his or her work. If you direct or control the result of the work but not the means and methods of getting it done, the worker is probably an independent contractor. But if you instruct the worker on how, when, or where to do the work, or what tools or equipment to use, or if you provide training, the IRS will likely classify the worker as an employee. The same is true if you provide benefits such as health insurance. On the other hand, if the worker serves several customers or clients—not just your business alone—the balance may shift toward an independent contractor relationship.

EXAMPLE: Liz has a bookkeeping service that she runs out of her home. She works for several small businesses. Every week, she stops by each of her clients' businesses to pick up the raw data she needs to do her work. Then she returns home to prepare invoices, compute business taxes, balance the books, and provide financial statements. She bills each client at the end of the month based on the amount of work she's done. Liz is an independent contractor.

EXAMPLE: Joe is a bookkeeper. He works half-time at Hali's company, Fleetwood Security Services. The company provides a workstation for Joe, along with a computer, bookkeeping software, and all supplies. Hali closely supervises Joe and pays him a set amount of $1,600 every two weeks. Joe is an employee.

Disadvantage of hiring an independent contractor. Be aware that you'll probably have to pay an independent contractor a higher hourly rate than you would pay an employee doing the same job. The reasoning for this is that you will not be providing the worker with traditional benefits and amenities, such as health insurance or a workspace; the independent contractor will be responsible for securing and paying for them, instead.

Advantages of hiring an independent contractor. Hiring an independent contractor can get you the services of an experienced, hopefully low-maintenance worker while saving on overhead and paperwork.

If a worker truly is an independent contractor, you don't have to worry about payroll taxes, workers' compensation, or unemployment fees, or even about providing traditional employee benefits such as vacation. And as mentioned, you generally won't need to provide the worker with a workspace, equipment, or supplies.

In addition, you might enjoy the flexibility of the arrangement, and the fact that you don't have an ongoing commitment to the worker. You can pay the worker for services only as needed, rather than having to write paychecks even when business is slow.

SEE AN EXPERT

Because misclassifying a worker as an independent contractor can be costly, consider consulting a lawyer or accountant for guidance if your situation seems unclear.

RESOURCE

For in-depth coverage of hiring independent contractors, see *Working with Independent Contractors*, by Stephen Fishman (Nolo). It explains in detail how to determine a worker's status, and provides an agreement you can use if you conclude that it's legally safe to treat the worker as an independent contractor. For an explanation of the pros and cons of hiring independent contractors, go to www.nolo.com/article.cfm/ ObjectID/B598DE79-D4CC-4FE0-A9B8A78C3CADC28B.

You can also consult IRS Publication 15-A, *Employer's Supplemental Tax Guide,* available online at www.irs.gov.

If you're still unsure about whether a person meets the IRS criteria, you can complete and submit IRS Form SS-8, *Determination of Worker Status for Purposes of Federal Employment Taxes and Income Tax Withholding*, also available at the IRS website.

Referring Out Excess Business

If you have more business coming your way than you can comfortably handle, one solution may be to make a referral arrangement with a business similar to yours that can deliver comparable goods or services to meet the needs of your potential customers or clients. As commonly structured, you and the other business owner would agree to pay a referral fee for business you send one another. This can be a flat fee for each customer you refer, a commission based on a percentage of what the customer pays, or a combination of both.

Disadvantage of referring out excess business. The negative side is obvious: You won't be able to earn the full profits from the excess business.

Advantages of referring out excess business. The referral arrangement might allow you to reap some benefit in the form of goodwill: Some potential customers or clients may appreciate that you pointed them in the right direction. And in the future, when your business has grown, they may return to you.

Also, while you pay nothing out-of-pocket, you may get a referral fee—and actually make some money on the business you are forced to turn away.

Finally, you don't have to supervise a worker or tend to employment paperwork.

Comparing Your Options

Now that you know some of the alternative options to hiring a worker as an employee, the following chart may help you decide whether one of them fits your needs.

When You Need Help: Comparing Your Options		
Possible Solution	**Advantages**	**Disadvantages**
Hiring an employee	Employee works for your business exclusively	May take time and effort to find the right person
	Likely to be loyal and hard-working	Commitment to write paychecks regularly
	Employee can be trained to meet your specific needs	Expense of payroll taxes and workers' compensation insurance
	No IRS issue regarding proper classification	
Adding a co-owner	Co-owner likely to work hard	Profits must be shared
	No cash outlay	Increases the possibility of management disagreements
	Co-owner may bring cash into the business	Possible legal expense in creating new ownership relationship
	No employment taxes	
	No workers' compensation or unemployment costs	
Leasing an employee	Avoids time and expense of an employee search	Premium prices charged to cover leasing agency's business costs
	No employee paperwork	Reduced worker loyalty
	Agency handles payroll, including employment taxes	
	Agency handles workers' compensation and unemployment costs	
	Easy to end the relationship	

When You Need Help: Comparing Your Options (cont'd)		
Possible Solution	**Advantages**	**Disadvantages**
Retaining an independent contractor	Ability to use the worker on an as-needed basis	Little control over how the job gets done
	Easy to end the relationship	Reduced worker loyalty
	No employee paperwork	Higher cost
	No employment taxes	IRS may determine that the worker is really an employee
	Avoids workers' compensation and unemployment costs	
Referring out excess business	Chance to make some money on the excess business	Loss of customer's or client's current business
	May earn customer's or client's gratitude for the referral, leading to future business	May lose the customer or client forever
	No cash outlay	
	No employee paperwork	
	No supervisory duties	
	Chance to build valuable relationships with other businesses	

Assessing the Cost of Hiring an Employee

Ideally, hiring an employee will free up some of your time and energy and increase your business's profitability. But before you act on this vision, it would be wise to do a realistic cost-benefit analysis to ascertain whether it makes financial sense to bring an employee on board.

It's impossible to know exactly how much adding an employee will help raise your profits—for example, if it would enable you to take on a promising new client or keep your business open on weekends—so you'll have to make an informed guess. Then comes the other part of the equation: estimating how much it will cost you to hire someone.

Some expenses will be the same, no matter what the nature of your business. These include:

• standard wages

• the employer's share of Social Security and Medicare taxes

• unemployment tax, and

• workers' compensation insurance.

Beyond these basic costs, you may want to offer health care insurance or other benefits. (See Chapter 4 for a complete discussion.)

In addition, you might cover the cost of other tangible work-related expenses, such as:

• business cards

• work stations

• computers

• phones

• pagers

• parking spaces

• vehicles

• uniforms

• professional dues

• seminars or other educational opportunities, and

• travel expenses.

Businesses differ greatly, so you will not likely need to cover all the costs on the list. And you will likely get the chance to make sure the working relationship is solid and beneficial before extending beyond the basics to covering an employee's expenses such as professional dues and educational costs.

Several other factors may help offset the costs of having an employee. The first is that you may be able to make more efficient use of existing equipment. For example, if you are only using a truck half time to make deliveries in your current business, you may use the truck full-time once you hire an employee—and can double the amount of deliveries you make to produce more income.

The second factor is that having a $12-an-hour employee perform some of the work that you're currently doing can free you up to do more work that will bring in $40 an hour. Finally, employment costs are deductible from your business's gross income when computing its income tax, which reduces the amount of the tax you will owe. (See Chapter 12 for a detailed explanation of deducting employee expenses.)

The key idea is that you should run the numbers—mostly estimates at this point—to test whether hiring an employee will help or hurt your bottom line.

TIP

Keeping it flexible. By observing some simple precautions discussed below, you'll be free to end the employment relationship if you find that the financial burdens outweigh the benefits. This helps limit the risk of making a costly error by taking on an employee. If things don't go as planned, you can bail out.

Myths About Being an Employer

Many business owners wait longer than they should to hire help because of misconceptions—myths, actually—about the nature of being an employer. Three common myths are examined below, along with the reasons why fears associated with them are usually overblown.

Myth 1: Firing an Employee is Legally Risky

You may have read newspaper and magazine accounts of employers who fired an employee, got sued for wrongful discharge, and had to pay tens of thousands of dollars in damages. Better to run the business by yourself, you may think, than be exposed to such a nasty lawsuit. But the reality is that the law is quite favorable to employers.

In nearly every state, the basic legal rule is that employment is "at will." This means that you are generally free to fire an employee at any time for any reason—or without any reason. You don't have to show that you had good cause to let the employee go. If you treat your employee fairly and give reasonable warning that his or her performance is not up to par, you needn't lose sleep over the possibility of a lawsuit; the risk is minimal. (For details on troubleshooting problems with employees, see Chapter 13.)

Myth 2: Employers Must Comply With Dozens of Regulations

If you're like most small business owners, you bristle when the subject of government regulation comes up. That's understandable. As an entrepreneur, you're likely to be a free spirit who likes to operate without handcuffs.

Chances are, however, that even if you have no employees on staff, your business is already controlled by a number of local and state regulations. For example, if you have anything to do with food preparation, you may need a health department permit—and may have to put up with periodic inspections. If you're involved in construction work, you probably have to get municipal permits for each project you undertake. And in some types of businesses you may be required to secure a trade or professional license from the state.

The burdens of complying with laws and regulations will scarcely increase once you become an employer. There are some simple paperwork requirements during the hiring phase. (See Chapter 7 for complete details.) Once your employee is on board, you'll have to account for and send in payroll taxes. (See Chapter 11.) In addition, you'll have to observe the minimum wage requirements, including overtime pay rules. (See Chapter 3.) And you'll have to comply with your state's workers' compensation law, which amounts to no more than buying insurance. (See Chapter 9.) But in most cases, that's it.

Your Main Legal Responsibilities as an Employer

A single-employee business must comply with the legal mandates listed below. Each is covered in detail in later chapters.

Wages and hours. Generally, you must pay employees at least the minimum wage, plus time-and-a-half for overtime work. (See Chapter 3.)

Nondiscrimination. You must not discriminate against an applicant or employee on the basis of race. This applies throughout the employment process—including hiring, pay, benefits, and firing. In some states, you must also avoid discriminating on the basis of gender, religious beliefs, or national origin. (See Chapter 2.)

Credit investigations. You must get written consent from an applicant before you order a credit report. Then, if you don't hire the applicant, you must give certain information about the report. (See Chapter 6.)

Worker verification. You must verify that your employee is legally authorized to work in the United States. (See Chapter 7.)

New hire reporting. You must report your new hire to a state registry so that parents who aren't paying required child support can be located. (See Chapter 7.)

Payroll taxes. You must withhold income tax and Social Security and Medicare taxes from your employee's paycheck. Also, you must pay the employer's share of Social Security and Medicare taxes. (See Chapter 10.)

Safe workplace. You must provide safe working conditions for your employee. (See Chapter 9.)

Workers' compensation insurance. You must buy workers' compensation insurance in case your employee is injured on the job. (See Chapter 9.)

For more in-depth information on these topics, see *The Essential Guide to Federal Employment Laws,* by Lisa Guerin and Amy DelPo (Nolo).

Myth 3: Employers Must Pay for Costly Benefits

Health care insurance, employer-funded retirement accounts, paid vacation time: These can all loom large as burdensome expenses. But the fact is that these benefits are not required by federal law, and hardly ever specified by state law. You may choose to offer one or more benefits to your employee, which can help you attract and keep well-qualified candidates. But they're a choice—not a mandate. And most of the costs of these benefits are tax-deductible. (For more on this topic, see Chapters 4 and 12.)

Risks of Hiring an Employee "Off the Books"

It's no secret that some small business owners evade their legal responsibilities by hiring an employee "off the books." They pay the employee in cash and don't deduct income taxes or the employee's share of Social Security and Medicare taxes. In addition, they don't pay the employer's share of Social Security and Medicare taxes. They ignore the unemployment tax and they don't bother to buy workers' compensation insurance.

Skirting the law may be convenient for both the employer and the employee, and it may save both of them a few bucks. But it's a dangerous game. When caught, the employer faces tax liabilities and penalties. And if the employee is injured on the job and there's no workers' comp insurance in place, the employer may have to pay for the employee's medical expenses and some salary replacement.

The best course is to avoid informal hiring and to play by the rules.

Avoiding Legal Pitfalls

This chapter explains how you can avoid pitfalls that often permeate the employment relationship by heeding a few legal principles. The principles are easy to understand—and learning them will serve you well, as they come into play throughout the hiring process and beyond.

These legal rules can control many phases of employment, including:

- writing job descriptions
- preparing job application forms
- advertising job openings
- interviewing applicants
- making job offers
- putting together employee handbooks
- calculating employee pay, and
- firing employees.

By observing a number of precautions, you can greatly reduce the chances of accidentally creating legal problems for yourself and your business.

Preserve Your Right to End the Relationship

In nearly all states, an employer has a broad right to fire an employee for any reason or no reason at all. That is the basic definition of the legal doctrine known as employment at will.

Montana Marches to a Different Drummer

In Montana, a statute called the Wrongful Discharge From Employment Act trumps the at-will rule. In that state, the at-will principle applies only during an employee's probationary period—which is six months, unless the employer specifies a different probationary period while hiring.

After that, the employer must have "good cause" to fire the employee. The Montana statute defines good cause as "reasonable job-related grounds for dismissal based on a failure to satisfactorily perform job duties, disruption of the employer's operation, or other legitimate business reason."

As examples, Montana courts have held that an employer was justified in firing a worker who:

- took $350 from the till for a gambling junket in violation of a company policy prohibiting employees from borrowing company funds for personal use
- called several of his supervisors and suggested they pack their bags for a "little trip to hell" after being suspended for sexually harassing and intimidating his coworkers
- failed to implement new procedures and delayed completing job tasks, even after being warned, and
- told a husband and wife that the used car they bought from his employer's dealership was "a piece of [expletive deleted]."

In all these cases, the courts found that the former employee's actions gave the employer the required good cause to be fired.

Of course, it's always a better business practice—and more fair to an employee—if you have a good reason for any firing. If your reason is the employee's subpar performance, warn the employee as early as possible that his or her job is on the line. Given a warning and some specific guidance, many employees are able to improve—a win all around. (See Chapter 13 for more on this.)

Even if the employment relationship doesn't work out and you have to end it, the employee will be less likely to feel you've been unfair if the firing doesn't come as a complete surprise. And fairness is an important goal. For one thing, it's unpleasant to have a disgruntled former employee bad-mouthing you and your business. Beyond that, if you and the fired worker get into a legal dispute, it's better strategically if your actions don't appear to be arbitrary and callous.

Still, it is wise to take specific steps to preserve your legal right to fire an employee. In an interview, for example, be careful not to promise or imply that the job is secure. And if you make a written job offer, emphasize in it that employment will be on an at-will basis. Don't say something to an applicant or newly hired employee that might create ambiguity on this point. (See the discussion of "Implied Employment Contracts," below, and Chapter 6 for details.)

Possible Limits on Firing

As broad as the at-will employment rule is, as explained below, there are some limits to it. Generally, it will not apply, and you may not be allowed to fire a worker freely, if you promise job security orally or in writing or if you conduct your business unfairly or illegally.

Written Employment Contracts

The at-will rule doesn't apply if you and your employee have signed a contract specifically promising him or her job security. Such written employment contracts are extremely rare in small businesses—and many of those that do exist may have been offered unknowingly.

A typical written employment contract might specify that you can only fire the employee for good cause, which the contract may define, for example, as dishonesty, failure to meet sales goals, or habitual tardiness. In such cases, you will be held to the words of the signed contract, and so be legally able to fire the employee only for the specific reasons mentioned.

Implied Employment Contracts

While it is somewhat rare, two people can also form an "implied employment contract," which need not be in writing. In general, contracts are formed when people exchange promises with one another, or when one person acts in reliance on a promise made by another person. Sometimes, creating a reasonable expectation can amount to a promise. In the employment world, a contract may be implied when an employer creates an expectation of job security—and relying on that expectation, an applicant takes the job.

For example, you may become bound by an implied contract based on statements made in a poorly drafted employee manual, job offer, job description—or unwittingly, while being upbeat and optimistic during a job interview. If you have an implied contract that includes job security, the at-will rule does not apply. (See "Pitfalls of Making Promises," below, for tangible tips on avoiding this problem.)

 TIP

Have your employee acknowledge in writing that the employment is at-will. You can include a statement emphasizing that the employment is at-will in your employment application form or in a separate document. An increasing number of states require that an employer produce a written acknowledgement of an at-will relationship to overcome an employee's claim that there was an implied contract.

Illegal Discrimination

The at-will rule does not apply if you illegally discriminate when firing an employee. (See "Follow Anti-Discrimination Guidelines," below, for details.)

Public Policy Restrictions

The at-will rule doesn't apply if the firing would violate public policy. A public policy is usually created by a statute—that is, a law passed by a legislature. But sometimes it's established by a court.

For example, depending on the law in your state, it may be a violation of pubic policy to fire someone for:

- taking time off to vote or serve on a jury
- filing a workers' compensation claim
- reporting illegal activity to the authorities, also called whistleblowing, or
- refusing to file phony reports with a state agency.

The idea behind a public policy violation is that the employer's action harms the general public—not just the individual employee.

If you use common sense and deal fairly and honestly with your employee, you shouldn't run into trouble.

Good Faith and Fair Dealing

Courts in a few states have ruled that every employment relationship comes with an implied promise that an employer will treat employees fairly. In applying this principle, courts seem particularly protective of long-term employees who are arbitrarily fired and stand to lose retirement benefits. For example, a court is likely to find it unfair if, without good cause, you fire a worker who has put in 20 years of service.

As with the public policy exception, operating your business fairly and honestly should easily keep you in safe legal territory.

RESOURCE

For general information on the public policy and good faith and fair dealing exceptions to the at-will employment rule, see "The Employment-at-Will Doctrine: Three Major Exceptions," at www.bls.gov/opub/mlr/2001/01/art1full.pdf.

For specific local information, consult your state's labor department. You will find contact information at www.dol.gov/esa/contacts/state_of.htm.

Pitfalls of Making Promises

In enticing people to apply for a job, it is a natural tendency to paint a glowing picture of what lies ahead, putting the job in the best possible light, which may also include a description of possible job benefits. (See Chapter 4 for more on possible benefits to offer.)

All that is fine—up to a point. Problems may arise if you promise or imply a job benefit, because a court may later determine that you've made a legally binding commitment to deliver it. Any number of statements can later be determined to be legally enforceable promises.

In a job description, for example, statements such as these can be interpreted as promises:

- "Good starting salary, with periodic increases."
- "Chance to boost your income through overtime work."

And in interviewing applicants or making a job offer, you might be tempted to include specific descriptions of workplace benefits, such as:

- "After six months, you'll be eligible for health care benefits."
- "If you do a good job, you'll have a chance to become a co-owner."
- "Next year, you'll get a substantial salary increase."
- "I can't pay a whole lot right now, but I will teach you how to operate the latest technology in this field."

An applicant may interpret such statements as tangible promises of job benefits and rely on them in accepting your job offer. And in the name of fairness, a court considering the situation may rule that you must honor the promise you made when enticing the applicant to come work for you.

Here, the lesson is simple and obvious: To avoid binding promises, don't oversell the job. Watch what you say, be mindful of how written documents describe the terms and conditions of employment, and think about how an applicant might logically interpret them. If a statement could be taken for a promise, you may be stuck with it. Know in advance what benefits you are prepared to provide. Then, if the prospective employee asks about vacations, you can answer the question with specific information.

By contrast, you may not be sure if you'll be paying a bonus, or how much you might be able to afford. In such cases, if a prospective employee asks about how big a bonus he or she will get, your response might be: "I'm not sure there will be a bonus, but if I decide you've earned one, the amount will be based on your performance and how well the business has done." That way, you will not have raised the person's expectations unfairly.

Follow Anti-Discrimination Guidelines

Several federal laws prohibit discrimination in all stages of employment—from hiring through firing. For example, the Civil Rights Act of 1964 outlaws discrimination based on color, race, religion, gender, or national origin; sexual harassment in the workplace is prohibited as a variety of illegal gender discrimination. Other federal laws prohibit discrimination based on pregnancy, citizenship, disability, or age if the person is at least 40 years old. All of these laws apply only to businesses with at least 15 or 20 workers.

The only federal anti-discrimination law that directly affects a single-employee business is the Civil Rights Act of 1866, which prohibits discriminating against an applicant or employee on the basis of race. This applies to all aspects of the employment relationship—including hiring, pay, promotions, benefits, time off, discipline, and firing.

In hiring your first employee, for example, you would violate federal law if your ad or job description required applicants to be Caucasian, or if you quickly ended a job interview when you saw that the applicant was African-American. You would also violate federal law if you offered to pay an Asian applicant $13 an hour, but offered only $11 an hour to a Hispanic applicant.

Several states also have anti-discrimination laws that apply to a single-employee business. To learn which of these may affect your own business, see the chart below, "State Laws Prohibiting Discrimination in Employment." In addition, some city or county ordinances may also prohibit certain types of employment discrimination, including discrimination based on marital status or sexual orientation.

CAUTION

Watch how you count. In counting the number of employees to determine whether an anti-discrimination law or ordinance applies to your business, be aware that you—and any other owner—may be included in the total. Your business probably pays you a salary if it is set up as a corporation or LLC. If you're on your business's payroll, you are generally counted as an employee.

Regardless of whether your business is prohibited from engaging in certain types of discrimination, you may decide to proceed as if you are covered by the rule, which is generally a wise approach. This lets you focus on getting the best person for the job; you're less likely to be sidetracked by any of an applicant's characteristics that are not related to job abilities. Beyond that, Congress or a state legislature may expand the coverage of an anti-discrimination statute to include even the smallest employers. Getting in the habit of running your business fairly and not discriminating will make life easier for you if your business grows and you hire a sufficient number of employees so that you become covered by the broader anti-discrimination rules.

To meet anti-discrimination standards, your job description and any Help Wanted ads should not eliminate whole categories of people from the possibility of working for you, or discourage them from applying. So, for example, you should not state: "This job is for men only," or "Must be a U.S. citizen," or "Prefer church-going woman."

Also, beware of nuances in language that can be used as evidence of discrimination against applicants of a particular gender, age, or other protected characteristic.

A number of specific examples are listed below.

Don't Use	Use
Salesman	Salesperson
College student	Part-time worker
Handyman	General repairperson
Gal Friday	Office assistant
Counter girl	Retail clerk
Waiter	Server
Young	Energetic

TIP

When discrimination is allowed. In some very limited situations, religion, sex, or national origin can be considered a bona fide occupational qualification, or BFOQ, meaning that it is legally permissible to base an employment decision on whether an applicant has a particular trait. For example, gender is a BFOQ for a job affecting personal privacy—such as a locker room attendant at a health club. Similarly, being Catholic is a valid qualification for performing the duties of a Catholic priest. And Japanese nationality is a valid qualification for an American subsidiary of a Japanese company involved in international business transactions in which language proficiency and cultural background are important. But as mentioned, these exceptions are very rare.

Be careful, too, in setting requirements for education, skills, and experience. For example, if you arbitrarily require a college degree for people to be considered for a particular position, you may exclude a disproportionate number of applicants who are part a protected group that has relatively few college graduates. Of course, if there's a good business reason for requiring a college degree—for example, that it's necessary to obtain a license for a certain position—then it's fine to require it for your employee.

There are other times when a requirement that seems neutral can, in fact, be a form of discrimination.

EXAMPLE: Cal and Teresa, the owners of a packaging store, have decided to hire their first employee. In an effort to project a crisp, clean-cut image for their business, they decide that any male employee they hire must be clean shaven. Although such a policy may seem neutral, it may subtly discriminate against African-American men because a disproportionate number of them have an inflammatory skin condition that is aggravated by shaving. Unless a beard would affect job performance or safety, Cal and Teresa should abandon the no-beard idea.

A Fair Chance for Applicants With Disabilities

In avoiding potential discrimination claims, pay special attention to whether you're giving someone with a physical or mental disability a fair crack at getting the job. If you list a job duty on a job description or Help Wanted ad that's rarely going to be called for, you may deter a capable person from applying. (See Chapter 5, "Preparing a Job Description," for tips on this.)

Bear in mind, too, that it's often easy and inexpensive to accommodate a person with a disability to enable that person to do a particular job. Consider the following examples.

- **Person with arthritis whose hands get stiff and painful in cold temperatures.** *Possible accommodation:* Provide a space heater and better insulation around the windows.

- **Person with migraine headaches triggered by lighting.** *Possible accommodation:* Add filters to fluorescent lights and provide an anti-glare filter for the computer monitor.

- **Person with a hearing impairment who cannot hear a timing buzzer.** *Possible accommodation:* Install an indicator light to supplement the buzzer.

- **Person with diabetes who has reduced vision.** *Possible accommodation:* Provide brighter lighting in the work area.

- **Person who is paraplegic and uses a wheelchair.** *Possible accommodation:* Raise or lower work surfaces to a comfortable height.

- **Person with bronchial asthma who has problems with hot environments.** *Possible accommodation:* Install a window air conditioner.

For information on low-cost accommodations for a wide range of disabilities, go to the Job Accommodation Network's website at www. jan.wvu.edu. Also, in many cases, an applicant or employee with a disability can suggest a practical accommodation that won't break the bank.

Assuming you're located in a state or community that requires even a one-employee business to provide an accommodation to an employee with a disability, you need not take steps that would create a financial hardship for your business.

Reconsider the Legal Form of Your Business

If your business is a sole proprietorship or partnership, you may be able to avoid some potential legal problems or complications by switching it to a corporation or a limited liability company (LLC) when you become an employer.

As a sole proprietor or a partner, you're personally liable for business debts—a bank loan, for example, or a jury's verdict against the business. By hiring an employee, you increase the possibility that you'll also become liable for a business debt. That's because you'll be legally responsible for your employee's mistakes and misdeeds in addition to your own. Your employee, for example, may negligently injure a customer at your business place. If a verdict against your business exceeds your insurance coverage, you'll be personally liable for the excess.

By operating your business as a corporation or LLC, you can limit your personal liability to a great extent, which will help protect your nonbusiness assets such as your home, personal bank account, and stock investments. The only downsides are the modest cost of creating the entity and a bit of additional paperwork.

RESOURCE

For help in deciding the most suitable legal form for your business, see *Legal Guide for Starting & Running a Small Business,* by Fred S. Steingold (Nolo), and *LLC or Corporation: How to Choose the Right Form for Your Business,* by Anthony Mancuso (Nolo).

SEE AN EXPERT

Still uncertain? If, after doing a bit of investigating on your own, you remain uncertain about the best form for your business, a lawyer or CPA can help you weigh the pros cons of forming either a corporation or an LLC.

State Laws Prohibiting Discrimination in Employment

State/ Statutes	Private employers may not make employment decisions based on				
	Law applies to employers with	Age	Ancestry or national origin	Disability	AIDS/HIV
Alabama *Ala. Code §§ 25-1-20, 25-1-21*	20 or more employees	Yes (40 and older)			
Alaska *Alaska Stat. §§ 18.80.220, 47.30.865*	One or more employees	Yes (40 and older)	Yes	Physical or mental	Yes
Arizona *Ariz. Rev. Stat. Ann. §§ 41-1461, 41-1463, 41-1465*	15 or more employees	Yes (40 and older)	Yes	Physical or mental	Yes (according to A.G. opinion)
Arkansas *Ark. Code Ann. §§ 16-123-102, 16-123-107, 11-4-601, 11-5-403*	9 or more employees		Yes	Physical, mental, or sensory	
California *Cal. Gov't. Code §§ 12920, 12940, 12941, 12945, 12926.1; Cal. Lab. Code § 1101*	5 or more employees	Yes (40 and older)	Yes	Physical or mental	Yes
Colorado *Colo. Rev. Stat. §§ 24-34-301, 24-34-401, 24-34-402, 27-10-115, 24-34-402.5*	One or more employees	Yes (40 to 70)	Yes	Physical, mental, or learning	Yes
Connecticut *Conn. Gen. Stat. Ann. §§ 46a-51, 46a-60, 46a-81a, 46a-81c*	3 or more employees	Yes (40 and older)	Yes	Present or past physical (including blindness), mental, learning, or mental retardation	Yes
Delaware *Del. Code Ann. tit. 19, §§ 710, 711, 724*	4 or more employees	Yes (40 and older)	Yes	Physical or mental	Yes

Gender	Marital status	Pregnancy, childbirth and related medical conditions	Race or color	Religion or creed	Sexual orientation	Genetic information	Additional categories
Yes	Yes (includes changes in status)	Yes (includes parenthood)	Yes	Yes			Mental illness
Yes			Yes	Yes		Yes	
Yes		Yes	Yes	Yes		Yes	
Yes	Yes	Yes	Yes	Yes	Yes	Yes	Medical condition; political activities or affiliations
Yes		Yes	Yes	Yes	Yes (including perceived sexual orientation)		Lawful conduct outside of work; mental illness
Yes	Yes (includes civil unions)	Yes	Yes	Yes	Yes (includes having a history of or being identified with a preference)	Yes	
Yes	Yes		Yes	Yes		Yes	

State Laws Prohibiting Discrimination in Employment, cont'd

State/ Statutes	Law applies to employers with	Age	Ancestry or national origin	Disability	AIDS/HIV
District of Columbia *D.C. Code Ann. §§ 2-1401.01, 2-1401.02*	One or more employees	Yes (18 and older)	Yes	Physical or mental	Yes
Florida *Fla. Stat. Ann. §§ 760.01, 760.02, 760.10, 760.50, 448.075*	15 or more employees	Yes	Yes	"Handicap"	Yes
Georgia *Ga. Code Ann. §§ 34-6A-1 and following, 34-5-1, 34-5-2, 34-1-2, 45-19-20 and following*	15 or more employees (disability); 10 or more employees (gender)	Yes (40 to 70)		Physical, mental, learning, or mental retardation	
Hawaii *Haw. Rev. Stat. §§ 378-1, 378-2, 378-2.5*	One or more employees	Yes	Yes	Physical or mental	Yes
Idaho *Idaho Code §§ 39-8303, 67-5902, 67-5909, 67-5910*	5 or more employees	Yes (40 and older)	Yes	Physical or mental	
Illinois *775 Ill. Comp. Stat. §§ 5/1-102, 5/1-103, 5/2-101 to 5/2-105; 820 Ill. Comp. Stat. § 180/30; 410 Ill. Comp. Stat. § 513/25; Ill. Admin. Code tit. 56, § 5210.110*	15 or more employees; one or more employees (disability)	Yes (40 and older)	Yes	Physical or mental	Yes

**Private employers may not make employment decisions based on**

Gender	Marital status	Pregnancy, childbirth and related medical conditions	Race or color	Religion or creed	Sexual orientation	Genetic information	Additional categories
Yes	Yes (includes domestic partnership)	Yes (includes parenthood)	Yes	Yes	Yes	Yes	Enrollment in vocational, professional, or college education; family duties; source of income; place of residence or business; personal appearance; political affiliation; victim of intrafamily offense; gender identity or expression; any reason other than individual merit
Yes	Yes		Yes	Yes			Sickle cell trait
Yes (wage discrimination only)							Domestic and agricultural employees not protected
Yes	Yes	Yes	Yes	Yes	Yes	Yes	Arrest and court records (unless there is a conviction directly related to job)
Yes		Yes	Yes	Yes		Yes	
Yes	Yes	Yes	Yes	Yes	Yes	Yes	Citizenship status; military status; unfavorable military discharge; gender identity; arrest record; victims of domestic violence

State Laws Prohibiting Discrimination in Employment, cont'd

State/Statutes	Private employers may not make employment decisions based on				
	Law applies to employers with	Age	Ancestry or national origin	Disability	AIDS/HIV
Indiana *Ind. Code Ann. §§ 22-9-1-2, 22-9-2-1, 22-9-2-2, 4-15-12-1, 4-15-12-2, 22-9-5-1 and following*	Six or more employees	Yes (40 to 70; applies to employers with one or more employees)	Yes	Physical or mental (15 or more employees)	
Iowa *Iowa Code §§ 216.2, 216.6, 729.6*	Four or more employees	Yes (18 and older)	Yes	Physical or mental	Yes
Kansas *Kan. Stat. Ann. §§ 44-1002, 44-1009, 44-1112, 44-1113, 44-1125, 44-1126, 65-6002(e)*	Four or more employees	Yes (18 and older)	Yes	Physical or mental	Yes
Kentucky *Ky. Rev. Stat. Ann. §§ 344.010, 344.030, 344.040, 207.130, 207.135, 207.150, 342.197*	Eight or more employees	Yes (40 and older)	Yes	Physical or mental	Yes
Louisiana *La. Rev. Stat. Ann. §§ 23:301 to 23:368*	20 or more employees	Yes (40 and older)	Yes	Physical or mental	
Maine *Me. Rev. Stat. Ann. tit. 5, §§ 19302, 4552, 4553, 4571- 4576, 23; tit. 26, § 833; tit. 39-A, § 353*	One or more employees	Yes	Yes	Physical or mental	
Maryland *Md. Code, Art. 49B, §§ 15, 16, 17*	15 or more employees	Yes	Yes	Physical or mental	
Massachusetts *Mass. Gen. Laws ch. 149 § 24A, ch. 151B, §§ 1, 4*	Six or more employees	Yes (40 and older)	Yes	Physical or mental	Yes

Gender	Marital status	Pregnancy, childbirth and related medical conditions	Race or color	Religion or creed	Sexual orientation	Genetic information	Additional categories
Yes			Yes	Yes			
Yes		Yes	Yes	Yes	Yes	Yes	Gender identity
Yes			Yes	Yes		Yes	Military service or status
Yes		Yes	Yes	Yes			Occupational pneumoconiosis with no respiratory impairment resulting from exposure to coal dust
Yes		Yes (applies to employers with more than 25 employees)	Yes	Yes		Yes	Sickle cell trait
Yes		Yes	Yes	Yes	Yes (includes perceived sexual orientation)	Yes	Gender identity or expression; past workers' compensation claim; past whistle-blowing
Yes	Yes	Yes	Yes	Yes	Yes	Yes	
Yes	Yes		Yes	Yes	Yes	Yes	Military service; arrest record

State Laws Prohibiting Discrimination in Employment, cont'd

State/ Statutes	Law applies to employers with	Age	Ancestry or national origin	Disability	AIDS/HIV
	Private employers may not make employment decisions based on				
Michigan *Mich. Comp. Laws §§ 37.1201, 37.1202, 37.2201, 37.2202, 37.1103, 37.2205a, 750.556*	One or more employees	Yes	Yes	Physical or mental	Yes
Minnesota *Minn. Stat. Ann. §§ 363A.03, 363A.08, 181.81, 181.974*	One or more employees	Yes (18 to 70)	Yes	Physical or mental	Yes
Mississippi *Miss. Code Ann. § 33-1-15*					
Missouri *Mo. Rev. Stat. §§ 213.010, 213.055, 191.665, 375.1306*	Six or more employees	Yes (40 to 70)	Yes	Physical or mental	Yes
Montana *Mont. Code Ann. §§ 49-2-101, 49-2-303, 49-2-310*	One or more employees	Yes	Yes	Physical or mental	
Nebraska *Neb. Rev. Stat. §§ 48-1102, 48-1104, 48-1001 to 48-1010, 20-168*	15 or more employees	Yes (40 and over; applies to employers with 20 or more employees)	Yes	Physical or mental	Yes
Nevada *Nev. Rev. Stat. Ann. §§ 613.310 and following*	15 or more employees	Yes (40 and older)	Yes	Physical or mental	
New Hampshire *N.H. Rev. Stat. Ann. §§ 354-A:2, 354-A:6, 354-A:7, 141-H:3*	Six or more employees	Yes	Yes	Physical or mental	

Gender	Marital status	Pregnancy, childbirth and related medical conditions	Race or color	Religion or creed	Sexual orientation	Genetic information	Additional categories
Yes	Yes	Yes	Yes	Yes		Yes	Height or weight; misdemeanor arrest record
Yes	Yes	Yes	Yes	Yes	Yes (includes perceived sexual orientation)	Yes	Gender identity; member of local commission; receiving public assistance
							Military status; no other protected categories unless employer receives public funding
Yes			Yes	Yes		Yes	
Yes	Yes	Yes	Yes	Yes			
Yes	Yes	Yes	Yes	Yes		Yes (all employ-ers)	
Yes		Yes	Yes	Yes	Yes (includes perceived sexual orientation)	Yes	Use of service animal; opposing unlawful employment practices
Yes	Yes	Yes	Yes	Yes	Yes	Yes	

State Laws Prohibiting Discrimination in Employment, cont'd					
	Private employers may not make employment decisions based on				
State/ Statutes	**Law applies to employers with**	**Age**	**Ancestry or national origin**	**Disability**	**AIDS/HIV**
New Jersey *N.J. Stat. Ann. §§ 10:5-1, 10:5-4.1, 10:5-5, 10:5-12, 10:5-29.1, 43:21-49*	One or more employees	Yes (18 to 70)	Yes	Past or present physical or mental	Yes
New Mexico *N.M. Stat. Ann. §§ 24-21-4, 28-1-2, 28-1-7*	Four or more employees	Yes (40 and older)	Yes	Physical or mental	
New York *N.Y. Exec. Law §§ 292, 296; N.Y. Lab. Law § 201-d*	Four or more employees	Yes (18 and older)	Yes	Physical or mental	Yes
North Carolina *N.C. Gen. Stat. §§ 143-422.2, 95-28.1, 127B-11, 130A-148, 168A-5*	15 or more employees	Yes	Yes	Physical or mental	Yes
North Dakota *N.D. Cent. Code §§ 14-02.4-02, 14-02.4-03, 34-01-17*	One or more employees	Yes (40 and older)	Yes	Physical or mental	
Ohio *Ohio Rev. Code Ann. §§ 4111.17, 4112.01, 4112.02*	Four or more employees	Yes (40 and older)	Yes	Physical, mental, or learning	
Oklahoma *Okla. Stat. Ann. tit. 25, §§ 1301, 1302; tit. 36, § 3614.2; tit. 44, § 208*	15 or more employees	Yes (40 and older)	Yes	Physical or mental	

Gender	Marital status	Pregnancy, childbirth and related medical conditions	Race or color	Religion or creed	Sexual orientation	Genetic information	Additional categories
Yes	Yes (includes civil union or domestic partnership status)	Yes	Yes	Yes	Yes (includes affectional orientation and perceived sexual orientation)	Yes	Atypical hereditary cellular or blood trait; military service; accompanied by service or guide dog; gender identity
Yes	Yes (applies to employers with 50 or more employees)	Yes	Yes	Yes	Yes (includes perceived sexual orientation; applies to employers with 15 or more employees)	Yes	Gender identity (employers with 15 or more employees); serious medical condition
Yes	Yes	Yes	Yes	Yes	Yes (includes perceived sexual orientation)	Yes	Lawful recreational activities when not at work; military status or service; observance of Sabbath; political activities; use of service dog
Yes			Yes	Yes		Yes	Military status or service; sickle cell or hemoglobin C trait
Yes	Yes	Yes	Yes	Yes			Lawful conduct outside of work; receiving public assistance
Yes		Yes	Yes	Yes			
Yes			Yes	Yes		Yes	Military service

State Laws Prohibiting Discrimination in Employment, cont'd

State/Statutes	Private employers may not make employment decisions based on				
	Law applies to employers with	Age	Ancestry or national origin	Disability	AIDS/HIV
Oregon *Or. Rev. Stat. §§ 659A.030, 659A.100 and following, 659A.303, 25.337*	One or more employees	Yes (18 and older)	Yes	Physical or mental (applies to employers with 6 or more employees)	
Pennsylvania *43 Pa. Cons. Stat. Ann. §§ 954-955*	Four or more employees	Yes (40 to 70)	Yes	Physical or mental	
Rhode Island *R.I. Gen. Laws §§ 28-6-18, 28-5-6, 28-5-7, 23-6-22, 12-28-10, 28-6.7-1*	Four or more employees; one or more employees (gender-based wage discrimination)	Yes (40 and older)	Yes	Physical or mental	Yes
South Carolina *S.C. Code §§ 1-13-30, 1-13-80*	15 or more employees	Yes (40 and older)	Yes	Physical or mental	
South Dakota *S.D. Codified Laws §§ 20-13-1, 20-13-10, 60-12-15, 60-2-20, 62-1-17*	One or more employees		Yes	Physical or mental	
Tennessee *Tenn. Code Ann. §§ 4-21-102, 4-21-401 and following, 8-50-103, 50-2-201, 50-2-202*	Eight or more employees; one or more employees (gender-based wage discrimination)	Yes (40 and older)	Yes	Physical, mental, or visual	
Texas *Tex. Lab. Code Ann. §§ 21.002, 21.051, 21.101, 21.106, 21.402*	15 or more employees	Yes (40 and older)	Yes	Physical or mental	

Gender	Marital status	Pregnancy, childbirth and related medical conditions	Race or color	Religion or creed	Sexual orientation	Genetic information	Additional categories
Yes	Yes	Yes	Yes	Yes	Yes	Yes	Parent who has medical support order imposed by court
Yes		Yes	Yes	Yes			GED rather than high school diploma; use of service animal; relationship or association with disabled person
Yes		Yes	Yes	Yes	Yes (includes perceived sexual orientation)	Yes	Domestic abuse victim; gender identity or expression
Yes		Yes	Yes	Yes			
Yes			Yes	Yes		Yes	Preexisting injury
Yes		Refer to chart on Family and Medical Leave	Yes	Yes			Use of guide dog
Yes		Yes	Yes	Yes		Yes	

State Laws Prohibiting Discrimination in Employment, cont'd

State/Statutes	Private employers may not make employment decisions based on				
	Law applies to employers with	Age	Ancestry or national origin	Disability	AIDS/HIV
Utah *Utah Code Ann. §§ 26-45-103, 34A-5-102, 34A-5-106*	15 or more employees	Yes (40 and older)	Yes	Physical or mental	Yes
Vermont *Vt. Stat. Ann. tit. 21, §§ 495, 495d; tit. 18, § 9333*	One or more employees	Yes (18 and older)	Yes	Physical, mental, or emotional	Yes
Virginia *Va. Code Ann. §§ 2.2-3900, 2.2-3901, 40.1-28.6, 40.1-28.7:1, 51.5-41*	One or more employees	Yes	Yes	Physical or mental	
Washington *Wash. Rev. Code Ann. §§ 38.40.110, 49.60.040, 49.60.172, 49.60.180, 49.12.175, 49.44.090; Wash. Admin. Code § 162-30-020*	Eight or more employees; one or more employees (gender-based wage discrimination)	Yes (40 and older)	Yes	Physical, mental, or sensory	Yes
West Virginia *W. Va. Code §§ 5-11-3, 5-11-9, 21-5B-1, 21-5B-3, 16-3C-3*	12 or more employees; one or more employees (gender-based wage discrimination)	Yes (40 and older)	Yes	Physical or mental, blindness	Yes
Wisconsin *Wis. Stat. Ann. §§ 111.32 and following*	One or more employees	Yes (40 and older)	Yes	Physical or mental	Yes
Wyoming *Wyo. Stat. Ann. §§ 27-9-102, 27-9-105, 19-11-104*	Two or more employees	Yes (40 and older)	Yes	Not specified	

Gender	Marital status	Pregnancy, childbirth and related medical conditions	Race or color	Religion or creed	Sexual orientation	Genetic information	Additional categories
Yes		Yes	Yes	Yes		Yes	
Yes			Yes	Yes	Yes	Yes	Place of birth
Yes	Yes	Yes	Yes	Yes		Yes	
Yes	Yes	Yes	Yes	Yes	Yes	Yes	Hepatitis C infection; member of state militia; use of service animal; gender identity
Yes			Yes	Yes			
Yes	Yes	Yes	Yes	Yes	Yes (includes having a history of or being identified with a preference)	Yes	Arrest or conviction record; member of national guard/state defense force/military reserve
Yes		Yes	Yes	Yes			Military service or status

Current as of February 2008

Setting the Pay Rate

Pay too little, and you won't be able to attract a talented, dedicated employee. Pay too much, and you risk ruining your business's financial health. This chapter will help you decide whether it's financially feasible to hire someone—and will guide you in striking the balance between a generous and a prudent price to pay for that help. After reading it, you should be able to come up with a specific dollar figure, or at least a range, to discuss with applicants once you start the hiring process.

There are some specific limits on how little you can pay. For example, you must at least meet the minimum amount required by state and federal law. And you'll need to figure in payroll taxes, including your share of Social Security and Medicare taxes, as well as state and federal unemployment taxes, as part of your total cost of providing pay. If you think an employee you hire may work more than 40 hours a week—or in some states, more than eight hours on a single day—you'll also need to understand the rules for computing overtime pay.

Of course, meeting the minimums of state and federal pay laws is just the starting point. If your business is flourishing, you may decide to pay more than the minimum—perhaps a lot more. Paying a wage that is more than the competitive norm not only helps you feel good about the business you're running, but allows you to attract a high-quality, enthusiastic employee. If a position requires somewhat sophisticated skills or experience, you will definitely have to offer more than the minimum wage to garner the attention of any viable candidates.

Minimum Pay and Overtime Requirements

Federal law requires you to pay at least $5.85 an hour—a minimum that will increase to $6.55 on July 24, 2008, and to $7.25 on that day in 2009. But several types of employees fall outside this rule. For example, if you're thinking of hiring a student for the summer, you might be able to take advantage of an exception in the law that allows you to pay a training wage of $4.25 an hour to an employee who is under the age of 20 during the first 90 days on the job. Other special rules apply to farm workers and transportation workers, as discussed below.

And if you plan to have an employee work late some nights or on weekends, beware that federal law also requires you to pay most employees time-and-a-half for each hour they work beyond 40 hours in a week.

The minimum pay and overtime requirements apply to employees, and not to independent contractors. (See Chapter 1, "Hiring an Independent Contractor," for a detailed discussion.)

RESOURCE

The U.S. Department of Labor's website contains helpful information on wage and hour laws at its website. Go to www.dol.gov/esa/whd/ and click on the topic on the left side of the screen. Or you can start with "Questions and Answers about the FLSA" at www.dol.gov/esa/whd/flsa/faq.htm.

CAUTION

Your state law may have stricter requirements than federal law. Many states establish a minimum wage that's higher than the federal minimum, and some have more stringent rules for employers concerning overtime pay. Where a state has rules that are more generous to an employee than the federal government's, you'll need to comply with the state rule. To learn the minimum wage in your state, go to www.dol.gov/esa/minwage/america.htm and click on the map, or check with your state's labor department for details. For more information on state labor laws, go to www.dol.gov/esa/programs/whd/state/state.htm and choose a topic.

Paying Less Than Minimum Wage

You can apply to the U.S. Department of Labor for a certificate that will enable you to pay certain workers less than the minimum wage—called a subminimum wage. This may appeal to you if you have a tight budget, or if you enjoy introducing people to the working world and nurturing their development, or providing an opportunity to people who have limited job options.

This certification program is intended to expand employment opportunities for:

- **messengers**—workers employed primarily to deliver letters and messages for delivery service businesses
- **apprentices**—workers at least 16 years old who are learning a skilled trade through a registered apprenticeship program
- **full-time students**—workers carrying a full-time class load who are employed in retail, a service industry, or agriculture
- **student learners**—students who are at least 16 years old—or at least 18 years old in a hazardous industry—and employed part time under a vocational training program
- **learners**—workers who are being trained for an occupation for which skill, dexterity, and judgment must be learned—and who, when first employed, produce little or nothing of value, and
- **people with disabilities**—workers whose earning or productive capacity is limited by a physical or mental disability.

Note that even though the U.S. Department of Labor may issue you a certificate, you must make sure your state law permits the subminimum wage.

Exceptions to the Minimum Wage and Overtime Rules

A common complaint about the federal wage and hour laws is that they are complicated to apply—especially the rules that make some employees exempt or partially exempt from them. As a starting point, you should know that there are some employees who are never exempt from the normal rules: They are labeled "nonexempt" employees.

For example, those deemed by law to be blue collar employees and first responders are always entitled to both the minimum wage and overtime pay specified in the federal law.

Blue collar workers perform repetitive operations with their hands that involve physical skill and energy. Examples include carpenters, electricians, mechanics, plumbers, craftspeople, construction workers, and laborers.

First responders are on the front lines of protecting health and safety. That includes police officers and firefighters, as well as some workers in the private sector, such as emergency medical technicians, ambulance personnel, and those who work with hazardous materials.

Employees Who Are Always Exempt

Some employees, who are labeled "exempt," are never entitled to overtime pay or a minimum wage. This odd assortment includes:

- employees of a seasonal amusement or recreational business such as a ski resort or a summer amusement park
- employees of a local newspaper with fewer than 4,000 customers
- newspaper delivery workers
- switchboard operators working for small phone companies, and
- some farm workers.

These exemptions have been carved out over the years to increase employment rates or to help keep specific industries solvent.

Employees Who Are Sometimes Exempt

There are several categories of workers who are exempt—that is, not entitled to federal wage and hour benefits—if they meet certain criteria. This is where the rules get especially complicated.

Executive, Administrative, and Professional Workers

You don't have to pay overtime or a minimum wage to an exempt white collar employee. This is someone who earns a salary of at least $455 a week ($23,660 a year) and performs executive, administrative, or professional work. Being paid a "salary" means the employee receives a preset amount each pay period, such as weekly or biweekly.

Executive, Administrative, and Professional Workers: Defined

Employers often misunderstand or misapply the federal regulations for who qualifies as an executive, administrative, or professional worker. The summary below will help guide you through the thicket.

Executive employees. Typically, an executive employee is someone you hire to run your business or one of its departments. The employee performs management duties such as planning budgets and monitoring legal compliance. He or she also directs the work of two or more full-time employees, or their equivalent, such as one full-time employee and two half-time employees. Given this requirement, your first employee cannot qualify as an executive employee.

Administrative employees. An administrative employee needn't supervise other employees, but must:

- primarily do office work or nonmanual work directly related to managing your business, and
- exercise discretion and independent judgment on significant business matters.

The U.S. Department of Labor lists several areas of work that it considers to be related to managing a business. The areas most likely to apply to a business with a single employee are accounting, purchasing, advertising, public relations, and administering a computer network or database.

Professional employees. A lawyer, accountant, doctor, dentist, engineer, teacher, scientist, architect, or pharmacist will generally qualify as a professional employee if the worker must use personal judgment in performing the job. The same is true of certain health care professionals, such as a registered nurse or dental hygienist.

RESOURCE

For more on this employee classification, see *The Employer's Legal Handbook*, by Fred S. Steingold (Nolo). You will also find good information at the U.S. Department of Labor website at www.dol.gov. The department also operates a confidential referral line at 866-487-9243 that assists employers in applying the standards to their businesses.

Highly Paid Employees

You don't have to provide a minimum wage or overtime pay to an employee who performs office or nonmanual work and earns $100,000 a year or more—which must include getting paid at least $455 per week paid on a salary or fee basis. To be in this category, the employee must regularly perform at least one of the duties of an exempt executive, administrative, or professional worker described above. This type of worker is also rare among very small businesses.

Outside Salespeople

An outside salesperson is exempt from minimum wage and overtime pay requirements. This is an employee whose main duty is making sales or obtaining orders or contracts for services or facilities. As another condition, the employee must regularly work away from your place of business.

Computer Specialists

You don't have to provide a minimum wage or overtime pay to an employee whose main duty involves:

- applying systems analysis techniques
- designing, analyzing, testing, or modifying computer systems or programs based on design specifications
- designing, analyzing, testing, or modifying computer programs related to machine operating systems, or
- a combination of these duties.

For this exemption to apply, you must pay the employee at least $455 a week on a salary or fee basis, or at least $27.63 an hour. This exemption doesn't apply to an employee who makes or repairs computers or related equipment.

Employees Exempt From Overtime Only

Some employees are entitled to the minimum wage, but not to premium overtime pay.

These include:

• taxicab drivers

• railroad and air carrier employees

• certain commissioned employees of a retail or service business

• employees who sell cars, trucks, farm implements, boats, or aircraft—as long as they don't work for the manufacturer and they sell to ultimate buyers

• certain parts clerks and mechanics who service vehicles

• announcers, news editors, and chief engineers of radio and TV stations in small towns

• movie theater employees, and

• farm workers. In addition, some farm workers are not entitled to the minimum wage.

Employees Who Get Tips or Commissions

Depending on the nature of your business, your employee may earn a certain amount of income from tips or commissions. In most cases, you will be allowed to pay less than the minimum wage and credit the tips the employee accumulates as part of that amount.

Tips

If your employee routinely earns at least $30 a month in tips, you can pay as little as $2.13 an hour. But the $2.13 plus the tips earned must bring the employee's hourly earnings to the minimum wage level. Otherwise, you have to pay enough so the hourly rate plus tips does meet that level.

Note also that many states have their own rules for paying tipped employees. For details, check with your state's labor department. You will find contact information at www.dol.gov/esa/contacts/state_of.htm.

Commissions

Commissions you pay to a sales employee can count toward the federal minimum wage—and in some cases, may take the place of any wages you must pay. However, if the commissions divided by hours worked don't meet the minimum level required by law, you must make up the difference.

Paying for Time Spent Not Working

Everyone needs a break once in a while. Federal law is less strict about requiring you to pay for breaks and other downtime than you might think. As an employer, you are free to figure out what is standard in your industry—and how much will keep your employees happy, healthy, and productive.

Try calling a trade association that serves businesses similar to yours and see what information is available. Most industries have one or more national trade associations, and there may even be an association at the state or local level. You can also check directly with similar businesses in your locale to learn how they handle employee breaks and other downtime.

Time Off

Federal law doesn't require you to pay your employee for time off, such as vacations, bereavement time, holidays, or sick days. However, some state laws control how you tally and accrue time off—and an increasing number of states and even municipalities have laws requiring sick leave.

In addition, some state laws require paid time off for jury duty and voting, among other things. Your state labor department can provide specifics. You can find contact information at www.dol.gov/esa/contacts/state_of.htm.

States Require a Variety of Employee Leaves

State laws require you to give your employee time off to attend to a wide range of civic duties—a number of them summarized below.

- **Jury duty.** This typically is unpaid leave, but a few states require you to pay a modest amount of wages.
- **Time off to vote.** Usually the employee gets two or three hours off with pay. But under most of these laws, time off is not required if the employee has two or three consecutive nonwork hours when the polls are open.
- **Military leave.** Generally, an employee is entitled to unpaid leave for military duty. The number of days varies from state to state.
- **Blood donation.** Several states require an employer to give an employee two hours of paid time off to donate blood.

In addition, several states have family and medical leave laws, requiring unpaid time off for an employee's family and medical needs, and for pregnancy, birth, or adoption. Most of these laws do not apply to employers with just one employee, but a few do.

For summaries of state laws requiring mandatory leave, see *The Manager's Legal Handbook*, by Amy DelPo and Lisa Guerin (Nolo).

Commuting Time

You needn't pay for the time your employee spends commuting between home and the normal job site. But you do need to pay for commuting time that's part of the job.

EXAMPLE: Cindy owns a computer repair service. She requires Asher, her technician, to stop by the shop each morning to pick up orders and testing equipment before he goes out on calls. Asher's workday starts when he checks in at Cindy's shop.

In addition, you need to pay for commuting time if you require your employee to go back and forth from your workplace at odd hours to take care of an emergency.

EXAMPLE: Peter hires Rocco as a maintenance worker at Sleepy Hollow Apartments. Rocco normally works 9 to 5 and is paid hourly. At 8 o'clock one evening, the apartment complex owner calls Rocco and asks him to come back to work to fix a plumbing problem affecting two units. It takes Rocco a half-hour to drive back to work, two hours to fix the problem, and another half-hour to drive home. Peter must pay Rocco for three hours: two work hours plus the extra hour of commuting required to attend to the emergency.

On-Call Time

An employee who has to stay on your premises while waiting for a work assignment must be paid for that time. This is true even if your employee is elsewhere, but can't use that time freely.

EXAMPLE: Pedro owns a business that installs and services audio systems in restaurants and catering halls. He hires Tina as his service assistant. Tina works during the day, Tuesday through Friday. Because it is especially crucial for audio systems to function properly on weekends, Pedro requires Tina to be on call as his back-up every Friday and Saturday evening. When she's on call, Tina must be able to get to any customer's place within 15 minutes, keep her cell phone free for calls from Pedro, and refrain from drinking alcohol. Because Tina isn't free to use her on-call time as she pleases, Pedro must pay her for the time.

> **TIP**
>
> **Respect your employee's private time.** Cell phones, pagers, and other electronic gizmos make it easier than ever to reach your employee any time of the day or night. You can reach your employee on the golf course, while dining at a restaurant, or while watching a favorite TV show. It's almost too easy these days to summon your employee back to work or send him or her on an after-hours mission.
>
> But for most employees—even workaholics or those striving to be accommodating—constant disruptions from an employer soon pall, even if the pay is good. So try to limit on-call duties to truly urgent situations. Your employee deserves ample time completely free of workplace worries.

Meal and Rest Breaks

Under federal law, you don't have to pay your employee for time spent to eat a meal or take a rest, as long as your employee is truly free from job duties during those periods.

About half the states, however, do require meal and rest breaks—and some of those states require that the employee be paid for one or all of those breaks.

Regardless of specific legal requirements, most small businesses give their employees a 30 to 60 minute lunch break each day, and two paid rest breaks of 15 or 20 minutes each.

Time Off for Expressing Breast Milk

Many nursing mothers express or extract breast milk through vacuum pump devices for feeding to a child at a later time.

Federal law doesn't require an employer to give an employee time off to express milk, but an increasing number of state laws do. Some of these laws mandate time off for breastfeeding as well. In some cases, these must be paid breaks. Several of these laws also require you to provide, or make a reasonable effort to provide, a room or other private area for the employee to use for expressing milk or breastfeeding.

Even if the law in your state doesn't yet require it, this is an accommodation that a nursing employee will certainly appreciate. For a 50-state summary of breastfeeding laws, go to www.ncsl.org/programs/health/breast50.htm.

Deciding How Much to Pay

For some jobs, you may be able to find a qualified worker who is willing to accept the minimum wage. But don't bet on it. If the position requires anything more than basic skills, or if you need a worker who'll have to commute or move for the job, you'll need to beat the minimum wage.

To decide on an appropriate wage, your first task is to gather as much information as you can about what other employers are paying for similar work.

Look at the website php.democratandchronicle.com/RocDocs/pay. You can use a pull-down menu to select the appropriate metropolitan area. Then, use a second pull-down menu to select a specific occupation. You will be given two averages for that occupation in your community. One is the *mean* average—the total annual earnings of employees divided by the number of employees in the sample. The other, and more useful figure, is the *median* average—the mid-point in earnings, meaning half of the employees earn more, and half earn less. For example, using this website, you'll quickly learn that in Ames, Iowa, the median annual salary for a baker is $25,820 and for a barista in a coffee shop it's $15,940.

Another valuable website is www.salary.com, where you can obtain pay information based on occupation and zip code. Basic information is free, but you'll have to pay for an in-depth, customized report.

You can also talk with other small business owners in your community who have filled similar positions. See what they're paying and what type of workers they're able to entice at that rate. A trade association serving your industry may also have figures on what employees typically are paid.

You may want to pay something more than the prevailing rate so you can be competitive. Also, by paying an above-average rate, you're likely to wind up with a more loyal employee—one who will work harder, and not be tempted to quit the minute another position becomes available that pays more.

And keep in mind that the wage rate isn't the sole factor in attracting a qualified and loyal employee. As explained in Chapter 4, there are other things you can offer, including good working conditions, free parking, flexible hours, and a chance to learn new skills—perks that cost you little or nothing. Job benefits can help keep you competitive.

EXAMPLE: Bernie owns a growing business that transfers videotapes and film to DVD. He has decided to hire an assistant, and learns that employers in the area are paying about $11 an hour to people with some technical skills. That sounds affordable to Bernie, but he want to attract the cream of the crop. So when people apply—mostly students from a nearby college— he points out many benefits he can offer beyond money: The person who is hired will work in a comfortable office and be trained to use the latest equipment. Also, Bernie's business is close to the college, and there is free, onsite parking. The job will take 20 hours a week, which can be flexibly scheduled around a student's class schedule. Bernie receives 25 applications and finally offers the job to Jean, a bright, hard-working student who eagerly accepts.

Hiring a Young Worker

Consider hiring a teenager. You may well benefit from the younger worker's energy and enthusiasm, as well as enjoy being a mentor to a future entrepreneur. Of course, the employee will lack experience, so you'll need to invest time in training and supervision. If you lack patience, this may not be the best choice for you.

Beware that federal rules are designed to discourage students from dropping out of school, and to also protect them from dangerous work. And state laws may impose still more restrictions on hiring young workers. Before you hire someone younger than 18, consult your state labor department to make sure you're on safe ground. Go to www.dol.gov/esa/contacts/state_of.htm for local contact information.

There are a number of basic age-related guidelines for hiring a person for a nonagricultural job.

- You may hire a person who is 18 years or older for any job, hazardous or not, for unlimited hours.
- You may hire a person who is 16 or 17 years old for any nonhazardous job for unlimited hours.
- You may hire a person who is 14 or 15 years old outside school hours in various nonmanufacturing and nonhazardous jobs. The employee can't work more than three hours on a school day, 18 hours in a school week, eight hours on a nonschool day, or 40 hours in a nonschool week. Also, work can't begin before 7 a.m. or end after 7 p.m.—except from June 1 through Labor Day, when evening hours are extended to 9 p.m.

Fourteen years old is the minimum age for most types of work. A person younger than 14 can deliver newspapers or perform in radio, TV, movie, or theatrical productions. And a person younger than 14 can work in a business owned by the parents—as long as the job isn't a manufacturing or hazardous job.

If your business involves preparing or serving food, be aware that a person who is 14 or 15 years old can only:

- cook on an electric or gas grill, not on open flames
- warm food in a microwave oven
- use a deep-fat fryer that automatically lowers food into hot oil, or
- dispense food from food warmers and steam tables.

For more details on these rules, as well as the rules for young agricultural workers, go to the U.S. Department of Labor's website at www.dol.gov.

Factoring in Employment Taxes

In addition to paying wages to your employee, you'll have to pay employment taxes to the federal government, including the employer's share of Medicare and Social Security taxes and the federal unemployment tax. The numbers are adjusted every year to keep up with inflation.

In 2008, the employer's share of Medicare tax is equal to 1.45% of your employee's paycheck. And your share of Social Security tax is equal to 6.2% of your employee's paycheck—although you can stop paying that once you've paid the employee $102,000 for the calendar year.

> EXAMPLE: Your employee earns $15,000 during the year, so your share of Medicare and Social Security taxes will total $1,147.50. If your employee earns $25,000 during the year, your share of these taxes would be $1,912.50.

You'll also be withholding similar amounts from your employee's paychecks as the employee's share of these taxes, and sending those amounts to the IRS, along with your share.

In addition, you'll have to pay a modest unemployment tax to the federal government, and typically to the state government as well. The federal tax is based on the first $7,000 you pay your employee during the calendar year; chances are, your annual bill for one employee will be $56 or less.

(Employment taxes are covered in detail in Chapter 11. That chapter includes information on how to properly deduct taxes from your employee's paycheck, compute your own tax obligation as an employer, and remit payments to the IRS.) ●

Considering Benefits to Offer

Offering an attractive wage is not the only way to motivate a qualified applicant to work with you. Applicants often look closely at the nonmonetary benefits provided. And once an employee is on board, these benefits can help create and maintain loyalty, not to mention good health and the capacity and incentive to work hard.

Still, for most people hiring a first employee, offering benefits is an option rather than a requirement. About the only exception is if your business is located in Hawaii, where virtually every employer must provide health care coverage.

Generally, you can choose what benefits to offer based on a balance of what you can afford and which benefits you think will best help attract and support a good employee. One hopeful note on the affordability front: You can deduct employee benefits on your business tax return.

This chapter will help you decide what benefits you might offer now or in the future. You'll discover that many benefits cost very little—and some very valuable ones cost nothing at all.

> **TIP**
>
> **If in doubt, wait.** While you do have to commit to the amount of wages you'll pay when you advertise or at least by the time you offer a job, you can hold off indefinitely on deciding whether to offer benefits. Another approach is to have benefits begin only after your first employee has been with you for a certain period—say, six months or a year.

Benefits That Cost Little or Nothing

In addition to benefits such as health care coverage or retirement savings contributions that cost money, there are other, less tangible benefits you can include in your employee's package.

Good working conditions are themselves a major benefit. For example, many workers will consider it a big boon if you can provide a well-lit and ventilated office or shop with a view, access to a kitchen for preparing lunch, or onsite care for children or pets.

Other free or low-cost benefits may include:

- **Flexible hours.** This lets your employee more easily juggle competing time demands, such as caring for children or older parents, or attending classes.

- **Free parking.** Parking that you provide on the premises or nearby can save your employee from the daily hassle of finding space on the street, having coins on hand to feed a meter, or paying for space in a public garage. (For more details on this, see "Parking and Commuting Costs," below.)

- **Opportunity to learn new skills and advance.** This can be a powerful incentive for an employee who looks ahead to more lucrative employment. It can help you attract an ambitious, motivated employee—the kind that can be a real asset to your small business.

- **Ability to work from home.** Telecommuting has never been easier. It may not work if you have a retail business that requires face-to-face contact with customers, but many office-based businesses can easily arrange for an employee to work at home, at least part of the time.

- **Paid or discounted membership to a health club or gym.** This can help keep your employee healthy and less stressed. There may a special rate available if both you and your employee sign up. Be aware, however, that unlike most benefits discussed here, you can't deduct the cost of this one as a business expense—and the cost of your employee's membership must be included as part of his or her income.

- **Allowing pets at work.** This can be a morale booster for an employee who is attached to a cat or dog. Of course, it probably won't be appropriate for some businesses—for example, those that sell or prepare food.

- **Supplying beverages and snacks.** This can help make your employee feel comfortable and experience less stress on the job.

- **Membership in a trade or professional organization, or a subscription to a work-related publication.** These will appeal to an employee who wants to get ahead in the business or profession. A not-so-incidental side effect may be that your employee will show ever-improving job skills.

- **Paid attendance at job-related seminars or workshops.** As with work-related memberships and subscriptions, you're helping meet long-term career objectives. At the same time, you're likely to wind up with a more skillful and productive employee as a result of the training.

- **Services that double as benefits.** If you don't incur substantial additional costs in providing a service to your employee that you provide to your customers, the tax law lets you do so. For example, if you have a catering business and a room that you rent to customers for their parties, you can let your employee use the room free for a party. The cost of the electricity and other such incidentals would not be substantial. You needn't treat the value of the room's use as part your employee's income.

> **TIP**
>
> **Having a hard time deciding?** You may be willing and able to put a certain sum of money toward employee benefits for the first year. But if you can't decide how best to allocate it, ask your employee for preferences. The worker may prefer to have the money go toward retirement savings rather than health care insurance or more paid vacation time.

What Other Employers Are Offering

A recent report by the Bureau of Labor Statistics revealed that:

- 61% of workers in private industry had access to retirement benefits
- 71% had access to medical plans, and
- 77% had access to paid holidays and paid vacation time.

The report also noted that by comparison, "quality-of-life" benefits—employer assistance for childcare, adoption assistance, long-term care insurance, flexible workplace, employer-provided home computer, and subsidized commuting—were relatively uncommon.

Keep in mind that the Bureau's statistics are for all businesses; the numbers may be different for smaller businesses.

For the full BLS report, go to www.bls.gov/opub/cwc/cm20071022ar01p1.htm.

Paid Time Off

An employee is likely to expect some time off during the year without having his or her normal paycheck reduced—and it is customary for a business, even a very small business, to meet that expectation. Paid time off for holidays is quite common, but you might also offer paid time off for vacations or when your employee is ill or must meet family responsibilities.

Holidays

Paid holidays are a common and valued job benefit. Be sure to specify your employee's paid holidays early on, preferably in writing.

Typical paid holidays include:

- Memorial Day
- Independence Day
- Labor Day

- Thanksgiving, and sometimes, the day after
- Christmas Day, and sometimes, Christmas Eve
- New Year's Day, and sometimes, New Year's Eve.

These holidays sometimes fall on a weekend. If your normal workweek is Monday through Friday, you'll need to decide whether to give your employee a day off on a weekday instead. Other holidays you might consider for paid time off include: Martin Luther King Jr. Day, Presidents' Day, Good Friday, Columbus Day, and Veterans' Day. The exact holidays you choose will partly depend on practices in your community.

Most small businesses are closed for the major holidays, but yours may not be—for example, New Year's Day may be a busy time for a catering business that provides food for football bowl parties. In that case, you might designate another day as a substitute, or let your employee choose one.

If your employee occasionally asks for time off to observe a religious holiday that is not on your schedule, you should usually be able to accommodate the request. Perhaps the employee can make up the time by working on one of your listed holidays.

Vacation

As with holidays, there is no law requiring you to give your employee time off for a vacation or to pay for that time. But it is good for your employee's mental health to have breaks from the daily grind—and it is customary for businesses to pay for some amount of vacation time.

One common formula for paid vacation time is for an employee to earn one day a month, up to a maximum of 10 days per year. The number of days earned can be increased after the employee has been with your business a while. For example, in the fifth year of employment, your employee might earn 15 days a year—at the rate of 1.25 days per month.

Some states have laws or regulations that affect how vacation time accrues. California and a few other states, for example, prohibit a "use it or lose it policy" under which the employee forfeits vacation days if they're not taken within a specified time. You can, however, place a reasonable cap on the number of vacation days your employee can accrue. Representatives at your state's department of labor can tell you the rules in your state. Go to www.dol.gov to find contact information for your local office.

Personal Leave

You might allow your employee to take one or two paid or unpaid days off each year for personal business, such as arranging for a mortgage or driving a child to college. You would not generally require your employee to account for this time off, but may ask to be given advance notice whenever possible.

Sick Time

Consider letting your employee miss up to five days a year for illness, and still be paid for that time. Giving your employee worry-free time to get better can lower the chances that you, or your customers or clients, will catch a nasty bug. San Francisco was the first to require employers to provide paid sick leave to employees, whether they work full time or part time. Similar laws and ordinances are under consideration elsewhere.

A Possible Cure for Sick Leave: PTO

Recent studies have found that compared to alternative rewards, time off ranks near the top of employees' preferences—even above cash bonuses, raises, and future career advancement. Recognizing this, a growing number of workplaces give employees a certain amount of Paid Time Off, or PTO, without labeling it vacation, sick leave, or personal leave; all three types of traditional time off are rolled into one figure.

For example, say a company's traditional system specifies that employees receive ten vacation days, seven sick days, and three personal days. The system is revamped, creating a PTO bank for each employee that accrues at a rate of 12 hours a month. That's 18 days a year that employees can use however they want.

Proponents of PTO, now embraced in nearly two-thirds of all larger workplaces, praise its flexibility, as it allows employees to claim and schedule time off from work when it best suits their needs. They also point out that PTO helps keep everyone more honest, as it obviates a worker's human tendency to fake a bout of the flu when his or her favorite team is playing a day game on the home field. Many employers also claim that PTO relieves them of the meddlesome duties of tracking and policing workers' time off.

And there is often an unexpected advantage for employees who leave a job with PTO on their slates: Unlike personal or sick leave, employers must pay them for time that has accrued but has not been taken.

There are possible disadvantages to the arrangement, however. Some research shows that workplaces with PTO policies give employees fewer days off, overall. And some lament that employees view PTO as a benefit and use all the time they are allotted—or regard PTO as vacation time and come to work when they are sick, jeopardizing their coworkers' health.

Source: *Your Rights in the Workplace,* by Barbara Kate Repa (Nolo).

Family and Medical Leave

Federal law requires larger businesses to grant unpaid time off while an employee takes care of family and medical needs. Some states have similar laws, a few of which apply to single-employee businesses as well.

Even if your business isn't required to provide such leave, you may decide to allow time off, paid or unpaid, so your employee can attend to the medical needs of a spouse, parent, or child, or deal with birth, adoption, or child care.

RESOURCE
For more information on state family and medical leave laws, see *The Essential Guide to Federal Employment Laws,* by Lisa Guerin and Amy DelPo (Nolo). You can also go to www.ncsl.org/programs/employ/fmlachart .htm for a state-by-state summary of these laws.

If you do offer time off work for any of the reasons outlined in this section, it is best to specifically limit the number of days an employee is entitled to take. And you may also want to set some ground rules. For example, you could require your employee to give you a specified amount of notice before taking time off for a vacation or personal business.

Health Care Coverage

You're not required to provide health insurance for your first employee unless you're in Hawaii, where state law requires it.

A few other states have health care requirements, but most don't apply to a single-employee business. In Massachusetts, for example, a company with 11 or more full-time employees must either contribute to a group health plan or pay an annual assessment to the state. In California, employers with 20 or more employees must pay a health care fee to the state for each employee who has worked at least 100 hours a month and has been with the company for three months. Health care legislation is pending in several other states.

> (!) **CAUTION**
>
> **Hawaii requires health coverage.** If your business is located in Hawaii, you must provide health coverage to employees who work at least 20 hours a week and who earn at least 86.67 times the state's minimum wage each month. Currently, the Hawaii minimum wage is $7.25 an hour. The means an employee currently needs to earn at least $628 (86.67 x $7.25 = $628) a month to be entitled to this benefit. The health care requirement kicks in after four consecutive weeks of employment.

Even though you may not be legally required to offer health care coverage, you might consider providing it. Recognize, however, that doing so can be expensive, and that not every employee will need it. Some people are already covered by the policy of a parent, spouse, or domestic partner. But many others don't have such coverage and will seek an employer willing to foot at least part of the bill. Realistically, if your business cannot afford to offer some degree of health care benefits, you may well lose the interest of some well-qualified applicants.

> (💡) **TIP**
>
> **Check for special small employer coverage.** A growing number of states offer health care plans tailored to the meet the needs of small employers—or run state agencies that can refer you to appropriate providers. Check with your local chamber of commerce to see whether your state offers a program geared to small businesses. In New York, for example, you can find affordable coverage through a program called "Healthy NY;" for more information, go to www.ins.state.ny.us/website2/hny/english/hny.htm.

If you do offer health care coverage, you have several options. You'll need to consider both the cost and how well the coverage will meet your employee's needs. A traditional plan lets the employee choose the doctor or hospital. The plan either pays the provider directly or reimburses the employee. But there's a growing trend away from traditional plans. Employers today tend to choose a health maintenance organization (HMO) or preferred provider organization (PPO) instead—either of which can save you money.

Alphabet Comparisons: HMOs v. PPOs

Here are the average annual insurance premiums that a small business was required to pay, as noted in a recent survey:

	HMO	PPO
Single coverage	$ 3,899	$ 4,505
Family coverage	$11,137	$11,793

Source: *Employer Health Benefits 2006 Survey,* by the Kaiser Family Foundation and The Health Research and Educational Trust. To see the full survey, go to www.kff.org/insurance/7527/upload/7527/.pdf.

In an HMO, a group of doctors and hospitals provide medical services for a fixed monthly fee. The employee must use the HMO doctors and hospitals unless it's an emergency or he or she obtains permission to go elsewhere. The employee chooses a primary care doctor from among the HMO's panel of providers, and must consult that doctor before being referred to a specialist.

In a PPO, a network of hospitals and doctors agree to provide medical care for specified fees. The employee seeking health care can choose among the PPO doctors and hospitals or go elsewhere, which usually requires paying a higher fee.

Whichever route you go, you'll need to decide how much of the premiums your business will pay. Among the choices are:

• paying the full amount

• splitting the cost with your employee—perhaps 80/20 or 50/50—using a payroll deduction for the employee's share

• paying the full cost, but requiring the employee to reimburse you for the extra cost of covering any dependents, and

• requiring the employee to pay the whole cost—which can still provide savings to the employee if you've arranged for inexpensive coverage through a group plan, such as one offered by a trade association.

You can also offer health care coverage through a tax-favored program such as a Health Savings Account (HSA), Flexible Spending Arrangement (FSA), or Health Reimbursement Arrangement (HRA).

RESOURCE

HSAs, FSAs, and HRAs are explained in detail in IRS Publication 969, *Health Savings Accounts and Other Tax-Favored Health Plans*, available online at www.irs.gov.

SEE AN EXPERT

Although many tax-favored plans may be cost-effective for your single-employee business, they are quite complicated. For that reason, they may not be practical. If you do decide to investigate these options, consider consulting a tax professional.

Retirement Savings

An employee interested in working for a very small business won't usually expect to be offered a traditional pension plan; those are becoming increasingly rare even among large companies. But employees who are worried about the future of Social Security are focusing more attention on how to save toward retirement—and you may be able to help ease your employee's concerns about the financial future.

In deciding whether to offer a retirement benefit, and what in what form, you need to keep one eye on the paperwork and administrative burdens—and the other eye on tax compliance. Ideally, you will be able to deduct your contributions, and the employee will be able to defer paying tax on your contributions as well as his or her own. Your best bet is to stick with a simple arrangement such as a 401(k) or an IRA-type plan.

RESOURCE

For more information on retirement plan options, see IRS Publication 560, *Retirement Plans for Small Business*. It's available at www .irs.gov. Also see *Choosing a Retirement Solution for Your Small Business*, which is available online at www.pueblo.gsa.gov/cic_text/smbuss/choosing-retirement/choosing-retirement.htm.

Other Benefits

There are several other benefits you may offer employees—and the tax laws make many of them especially attractive by allowing you to deduct their costs on your business return. As an added boon, your employee doesn't have to pay tax on these benefits. (See Chapter 12 for more on deducting employee-related expenses.)

Some of the benefits you might consider are described briefly below.

Group Term Life Insurance

You can buy group term life insurance for your employee, and are free to deduct the premium if the policy amount doesn't exceed $50,000.

Term life insurance pays the policy amount to the employee's beneficiaries if the employee dies within the term of the policy. Typically, the term is one year, but the policy can be renewed from year to year by paying a new premium. Your employee pays no tax on the premiums you pay. When you have fewer than ten full-time employees, you need to be part of a group plan that includes other businesses. Check with an insurance agent or trade association to learn what's available in your area.

Educational Assistance

You can pay—and deduct—up to $5,250 a year of an employee's educational expenses. This can include the cost of books, equipment, fees, supplies, and tuition.

The payments you make are not part of the employee's wages, so he or she is not taxed on this benefit. The assistance cannot be used for a course involving sports, games, or hobbies—unless the course is reasonably related to your business or is required as part of a degree program.

Allowable education expenses don't include the cost of tools or supplies, other than books, that your employee can keep at the end of the course, nor do they include the cost of lodging, meals, or transportation.

Dependent Care Assistance

You get a tax deduction for amounts you pay to help cover care for children and other dependents of your employee.

The payments must enable the employee to provide care for:

• dependents who are 12 years old or younger

• dependents who are physically or medically incapable of caring for themselves, or

• the employee's spouse if he or she can't care for himself or herself.

The amounts you deduct can be for bills you pay or money you reimburse to your employee for:

• at-home child care

• in-home care for elderly or disabled adults who live with your employee

• care at a licensed nursery school or kindergarten, or

• care at a dependent care center that provides day care for more than six people.

You can also pay for dependent care assistance at your place of business, though this often isn't practical for a business with just one employee.

There's a $5,000 annual limit on the amount you can pay and deduct as a business expense. And your employee can exclude up to $5,000 of these benefits from his or her gross income, or up to $2,500 if the employee and his or her spouse file separate returns.

A Look at the Benefits Being Provided

The Bureau of Labor Statistics (BLS) reports that employer assistance for child care is the most widely offered "quality of life" benefit—a term the Bureau uses to describe not only child care assistance, but also adoption assistance, long-term care insurance, flexible workplace, employer-provided home computer, and subsidized commuting.

The Bureau reports that in 2007, 15% of workers in private industry had access to employer-provided childcare assistance, which includes funds, onsite or offsite child care, and resource and referral services. For some workers, child care needs were covered by dependent care reimbursement accounts which set aside money to be used for expenses for child care, elder care, or services to a disabled dependent.

Finally, nearly a third of workers in private industry had access to dependent care reimbursement accounts.

The percentages are a bit lower in small businesses, but it's clear that across the board more and more employers are recognizing the importance of offering care assistance to employees.

For more on the BLS report, see "What Other Employers Are Offering," above.

TIP

Your employee may benefit more by taking the dependent care tax credit. The tax laws allow an income tax credit to many people who pay for dependent care. The size of the credit varies according to the taxpayer's income. Crunching the numbers can be mind-boggling. But in some cases, especially if your employee has low household income, he or she may be better off overall if you don't pay for dependent care but just pay more in wages. You might advise your employee to ask a tax professional whether the tax credit is the better way to go.

Adoption Assistance

You can assist your employee with adoption expenses—including adoption fees, attorney fees, court costs, and travel expenses while away from home. You can also assist with readoption expenses relating to the adoption of a child who was not a citizen or resident of the United States when the adoption process began.

The cap for tax purposes changes annually. The limit in 2007 was $11,390 for adopting an eligible child. The employee can exclude these payments on an individual tax return, though the amount of the exclusion is phased out for employees whose income exceeds $170,820.

Parking and Commuting Costs

If your employee drives to work, you can pay for parking near your business or near the location from which your employee commutes to work using mass transit, a carpool, or a commuter highway vehicle—such as a commercial van that seats at least six adults, not including the driver.

You can pay, and take a tax deduction, for this benefit. In 2007, the deduction for parking fees was set at up to $215 a month. If your employee uses commuter transportation, you can also help pay for a transit pass or trips in a commuter vehicle. The tax deduction limit in 2007 was set at $110 a month.

Your business can deduct these payments, and you need not include them as part of the employee's income.

EXAMPLE: To get to work, Rudy parks near a subway station and takes a subway train to a station where he boards a bus for the final leg of his journey. Rudy's employer can deduct up to $215 a month for Rudy's parking fees, and up to $110 a month for the transit pass that Rudy uses for subway and bus transportation. These payments are not part of Rudy's wages, and are tax-deductible by his employer.

RESOURCE

For more information on the tax treatment of fringe benefits, see IRS Publication 15-B, *Employer's Guide to Fringe Benefits,* available online at www.irs.gov. ●

Getting Ready to Hire

This chapter begins with an explanation of how to prepare a job description and a job application form, and then offers suggestions for finding potential employees. If you do not have a qualified candidate or two in mind for the job, you can reach out to potential workers using some of the methods described here.

Also, before you hire your first employee, you'll need to obtain an employer identification number, or EIN, from the IRS—and you may need to register with your state government as well. If you do not yet have an EIN, the last section of this chapter explains how to secure one.

> **TIP**
>
> **Heed the importance of putting it on paper.** There's no legal requirement that you prepare either a job description or an application form, but it's normally a good idea to do so. You might reasonably consider omitting these two steps if the job you have available is quite straightforward, and you don't have to learn a great deal more about the prospective employee; perhaps you've known the person for a while, or he or she comes highly recommended by a friend, colleague, or relative. Even then, however, a job description and application form will help clarify work matters for both you and the employee—and start the employment relationship on a solid footing.

Job Descriptions

A job description tells outsiders what the position entails and the qualifications you seek in the person who will fill it. A potential applicant needs this information to decide whether he or she is qualified to do the work and would enjoy doing it.

Benefits of a Job Description

As a small business owner, you understandably want to keep the pain of paperwork to a minimum—and might be tempted to skip writing a job description. But that would usually be a mistake. Better to take the time and get the hiring process off to a good start. And, as noted below, the effort you put into writing a job description will likely yield several additional benefits.

Clarifying the Job

Without thinking through a formal description, you may have just a vague idea of what the job will entail and the kinds of skills needed to do it. Writing a job description forces you to focus on exactly what you're looking for: what the job will consist of and the kind of person best suited to carry out the work duties.

Paving the Way for the Interview

A carefully considered and clearly written job description can make the interview process more productive. With a thorough job description in hand, you'll ask more precise questions—and provide better answers to questions applicants might ask you, especially about specifics of the job. During each interview, you can probe the applicant's experience and training for each of the job duties.

Avoiding Discrimination Claims

By giving an objective list of requirements for a particular position, a job description can help fend off potential claims of illegal discrimination.

A job description can be evidence, for example, that you considered all qualified applicants, without regard to their age, race, or religion. And by properly listing the essential job functions, you can go a long way toward defeating a claim that you discriminated against an applicant with a disability. (See "Preparing a Job Description," below, for more on this.)

Defining Expectations

A clear job description can help the person you eventually hire deliver a better performance. Once the employee is on the job, there will be no surprises.

TIP

Job descriptions may help ward off wage and hour claims. As explained in Chapter 3, most employees are entitled to overtime pay, but some—such as many salaried employees performing white-collar duties—are not. A properly worded job description can help you establish that an employee isn't entitled to overtime pay. In a close case, the duties stated in the job description may influence how the overtime rules are applied.

Personal Chemistry Isn't Everything

It's human nature to favor people you like. Understandably, you want to hire a person with whom you have good rapport. But you also need to guard against basing your hiring decision entirely on personal chemistry. It's a mistake to get swept away by personal traits that aren't necessarily tied to an applicant's abilities. And a carefully written job description will help you focus on an applicants' ability to perform the job duties.

Still, intangible personal characteristics—not always definable in a job description—can play a legitimate role in screening applicants and choosing one of them to become your employee. For example, you might give special consideration to a creative person who applies for a job as a gift wrapper, or to an applicant with a sunny disposition who wants to fill a sales position.

Preparing a Job Description

Preparing a job description is not as tedious as you might fear.

Most job descriptions include three basic elements:

- a summary of the job
- a description of the duties the employee will do, and
- a specification of the qualifications, skills, and experience required.

You may also choose to add a fourth part dealing with unique aspects of the particular job, such as special work hours.

RESOURCE

For in-depth guidance on preparing a job description, see *The Job Description Handbook*, by Margie Mader-Clark (Nolo). The book contains many sample job descriptions and comes with a CD-ROM that includes forms and templates that make it easy to write one.

Also, check out the free interactive program, Job Description Writer, at www.careerinfonet.org/jobwriter/default.aspx.

Job Summary

Your job description should begin with a brief summary of the job—usually a one- or two-sentence overview of what the employee will be doing.

If this doesn't come easily to you, practice by describing the open job to a friend or family member—and ask for feedback about whether your description is clear and concise.

TIP

Saving the first for last. You might want to save writing the job summary for last. You may find it easier to do once you've thought through and written out the details.

Job Duties

You'll next need to specify the meat of the matter by explaining more precisely what the job will entail.

Don't worry if you're not an experienced and confident writer. Start by making a wish list of everything you'd like your first employee to do.

For an office job, your list might include:

• answering the phone

• typing correspondence

• filing papers

- paying bills
- ordering supplies, and
- watering the plants.

For a food service job, it might specify:

- setting tables
- sweeping the floor
- writing daily specials on a blackboard
- picking up food supplies, and
- waiting on customers.

For a lawn maintenance job, you might write:

- ordering, picking up, and applying grass seed, fertilizer, and weed killer
- mowing lawns
- trimming hedges, and
- maintaining equipment.

In compiling your wish list, don't leave out any job duties because you think you may have trouble finding one employee who can do them all.

The Importance of Essential and Nonessential Duties

Sometimes, meeting all the requirements on the wish list seems like a tall order. Maybe there are many qualified people who can perform most of the duties required for the job, but a much small number who can do everything on the wish list.

So your next step is to divide your wish list into two categories: essential duties and nonessential duties. *Essential duties* are those that are an absolute must; the person you hire must have the skill and experience to perform those duties. *Nonessential duties* are those you'd like to have performed, but you'd be satisfied with an applicant who couldn't perform them.

EXAMPLE: Anton, who owns a number of apartment units, is seeking an assistant. He makes up this wish list of job duties that includes:

- showing vacant units
- performing credit checks
- preparing leases
- receiving security deposits and rent payments
- keeping records of deposits and rent
- making minor repairs
- dispatching maintenance contractors on major repairs
- assisting with evictions
- helping to prepare business tax returns, and
- working occasionally on holidays and weekends.

Anton thinks it over and decides that making repairs and helping with tax returns are not really essential. By listing these two duties as nonessential, he won't be turning away applicants who can handle the most important duties. This will increase the number of applicants. An otherwise highly qualified person who has no tax background won't be discouraged from applying, nor will an applicant who is unable to make repairs because of a physical disability.

> **TIP**
>
> **Separate and unequal job duties.** Treating nonessential duties separately helps extend job opportunities to applicants who have disabilities. This is especially important if your state's version of the Americans With Disabilities Act applies to single employee businesses. If a job duty on your wish list is rarely performed, separate it out as a nonessential duty. For example, an applicant with a back injury who cannot lift items heavier than 25 pounds should not be disqualified from a job if heavy lifting is hardly ever necessary. In that case, you would want to treat the ability to lift heavy items as a nonessential job duty.

Employee Qualifications

After you've settled on the essential and nonessential job duties, you can focus on qualifications—the section of the job description in which you list the skills, education, experience, and any license or special training you'd like the employee to bring to the job.

Again, if it's appropriate, you can divide this into two parts: basic qualifications that the employee must have—and other qualifications that are not required, but would be a desirable plus. In a job with financial duties, for example, an MBA degree might be useful, but not absolutely necessary.

> **TIP**
>
> **Be sure to include unique job requirements.** You can use a fourth section to describe any other features of the job that may be important to applicants. Maybe the employee will have to be on call occasionally, or do some out-of-town traveling, or attend a training seminar. These are all proper items to put in the separate additional section.

Writing a Description That Gets the Job Done

Margie Mader-Clark, an experienced human resources specialist, offers employers a number of Golden Rules for writing job descriptions.

- **Stick to the job.** Everything in the description must be directly related to the job. Emphasize job functions rather than a wish list of skills or personality traits. Avoid statements such as, "Sunny personality a must." Instead, focus on what the employee must do. For example, the job description might get this requirement across by noting, "Excellent customer service skills are a must."
- **Be clear.** Plain language beats fancy phrases every time.
- **Be reasonable.** Don't ask a future employee to do the impossible. One job description contained the broad condition: "Successful candidate must be available and on call 24/7." It would be better to specify what is true: "Employee will be on call and available for two 24-hour periods every two weeks."
- **Tell the truth.** If you exaggerate to make the job seem more appealing than it is, you may wind up with a disappointed employee.

Adapted from *The Job Description Handbook*, by Margie Mader-Clark (Nolo).

Distributing the Description

It's likely that a number of pairs of eyes in addition to your own will see the full job description you've crafted.

Certainly, you'll give a copy of the full description to people who express interest in the job so that they can determine if it's worth their time and effort to proceed to an interview. And you'll probably use a shortened version for any Help Wanted ad you run.

Beyond that, you may give a copy to friends and colleagues who may be able to point candidates in your direction. And you may want to post the job description on selected bulletin boards—at the supermarket, for example, or at a condominium clubhouse. If you turn to an employment agency for assistance, the job description will help the head hunter understand what qualities and qualifications you seek. And finally, if your business has a website, you can post the description online. In that case, your Help Wanted ads can refer interested people to your website for details.

But even if your job description never gets widely disseminated, the mere exercise of writing it will help you immensely in screening candidates and choosing which one to hire.

Sample Job Description

Below is an example of a job description that the owner an apartment rental business might write before hiring a first employee.

Job Description for Rental Assistant

The owner of 50 residential units is seeking a rental assistant. This is an opportunity to work in a relaxed atmosphere in the historic and highly popular Gas Light District. Diverse duties will keep the work interesting.

Job Summary

This employee will assist the owner with all phases of the rental process.

Essential Job Duties

- Show vacant units to prospective tenants
- Perform credit checks on prospective tenants
- Prepare leases for tenants who have been approved by owner
- Receive security deposits and rent payments
- Maintain accurate records of payments received
- Receive maintenance requests and dispatch maintenance contractors from approved list
- Assist with eviction proceedings
- Occasionally work on holidays and weekends

Nonessential Job Duties

- Perform some minor repairs
- Assist with preparing business tax returns

Job Qualifications

Basic Qualifications

- High school diploma
- Ability to work tactfully with a wide range of people
- Ability to use word processing equipment
- Valid driver's license
- Ability to work with minimal supervision

Additional Desirable Qualifications

- Bookkeeping experience—especially using QuickBooks or similar software
- Ability to make minor repairs
- Experience in the apartment rental business

Other Job Requirements

Leases typically expire at the end of a calendar month, and new leases start at the beginning of a calendar month. The rental assistant is expected to work longer hours during those turnover periods.

Job Applications

A job application enables you to learn about an applicant. A completed application form gives you information you need to decide whether the applicant has the background and skills required for the available job, and whether it makes sense to schedule an interview to get a closer look.

Benefits of Application Forms

Having jobseekers complete a well-prepared application form will allow you to reap a number of significant benefits and help hone your search for the most fitting candidate. Some of the advantages are summarized below.

Evaluating Applicants

First and most obvious, you can quickly scan a completed application to learn if an applicant meets your minimum requirements for the job. If not, you won't waste your time—or the applicant's—going through a meaningless interview.

Comparing Candidates

When several applicants are contending for a job, comparing their completed application forms can help you rank those in the running.

Preparing for an Interview

The information the applicant provides on the application gives you a solid basis for getting into specifics if you do an interview later.

Doing Background Checks

If an applicant seems like a promising possibility, the completed application gives you a foundation for doing a background check. You'll have the names and dates of the schools the applicant attended, and contact information for former employers. (See Chapter 6 for more on investigating applicants, including getting their prior written consent.)

Avoiding Discrimination Claims

As with the job description, the application form can help you establish that you're screening applicants based on legitimate business criteria, and that you're not illegally discriminating when filling the job.

Preparing a Job Application Form

As noted earlier, there's no legal requirement that you produce a job application form. And if you're well acquainted with the person you plan to hire, you may decide you don't need one. But in most other situations, you'll find it useful to have a form for applicants to complete.

CAUTION

Résumés are not enough. A jobseeker's résumé is not an adequate substitute for a completed application form—though it can be a useful supplement. The problem is that the résumé writer focuses on information the applicant feels you should know. But a résumé usually won't give you the details you believe are important for screening and investigating potential workers.

The best application forms simply focus on gathering information to help an employer decide whether the person applying for the job can perform it. It doesn't get into irrelevant information, but sticks to the skills and training the applicant would bring to the job.

A job application form should make no promises; instead, it should focus on soliciting information from the applicant. And to avoid getting into any areas that might violate an antidiscrimination statute or ordinance, the application should conform to several guidelines. (See the chart listing "Preemployment Inquiries," below, for a full explanation.)

Finally, the application form should make clear that if you hire the applicant, the employment will be on an at-will basis.

Using a job application form similar to the one suggested below should help you avoid the potential legal pitfalls at this stage of the hiring process. (See Chapter 6 for important legal guidelines on this.)

TIP

Another spot to reinforce employment at-will. The application form is another spot for you to make clear, and for the applicant to acknowledge, the possibility of being fired—and of being able to quit—for any reason or no reason. (See Chapter 2, "Preserve Your Right to End the Relationship," for specific details.)

Preemployment Inquiries		
Subject	**Lawful Preemployment Inquiries**	**Unlawful Preemployment Inquiries**
Name	Applicant's full name Have you ever worked for this company under a different name? Is any additional information relative to a different name necessary to check work record? If yes, explain.	Original name of an applicant whose name has been changed by court order or otherwise Applicant's maiden name
Address or duration of residence	How long have you been a resident of this state or city?	Do you rent or own?
Birthplace	None	Birthplace of applicant Birthplace of applicant's parents, spouse, or other close relatives Requirements that applicant submit birth certificate, naturalization, or baptismal record
Age	Are you 18 years old or older? This question may be asked only for the purpose of determining whether applicants are of legal age for employment.	How old are you? What is your date of birth?
Religion or creed	None	Inquiry into an applicant's religious denomination, religious affiliations, church, parish, pastor, or religious holidays observed
Race or color	None	Complexion or color of skin Inquiry regarding applicant's race
Photograph	None	Any requirement for a photograph prior to hire
Height	None	Inquiry regarding applicant's height (unless you have a legitimate business reason)
Weight	None	Inquiry regarding applicant's weight (unless you have a legitimate business reason)

Preemployment Inquiries (cont'd)		
Subject	**Lawful Preemployment Inquiries**	**Unlawful Preemployment Inquiries**
Marital status	Is your spouse employed by this employer?	Requirement that an applicant provide any information regarding marital status or children Are you single or married? Do you have any children? Is your spouse employed? What is your spouse's name?
Gender	None	Mr., Miss, Mrs., or any inquiry regarding gender; inquiry as to ability or plans to reproduce or advocacy of any form of birth control
Disability	These [provide applicant with list] are the essential functions of the job. How would you perform them?	Inquiries regarding an individual's physical or mental condition that are not directly related to the requirements of a specific job
Citizenship	Are you legally authorized to work in the United States on a full-time basis?	Questions about subjects below are unlawful, but the applicant may be required to reveal some of this information as part of the federal I-9 process: • Country of citizenship • Whether an applicant is naturalized or a native-born citizen; the date when the applicant acquired citizenship • Requirement that an applicant produce naturalization papers or first papers • Whether applicant's parents or spouse are naturalized or native-born citizens of the United States, and if so, the date when such parent or spouse acquired citizenship
National origin	Inquiry into languages applicant speaks and writes fluently	Inquiry into applicant's lineage, ancestry, national origin, descent, parentage, or nationality, unless part of the federal I-9 process in determining employment eligibility Nationality of applicant's parents or spouse Inquiry into how applicant acquired ability to read, write, or speak a foreign language

Preemployment Inquiries (cont'd)		
Subject	**Lawful Preemployment Inquiries**	**Unlawful Preemployment Inquiries**
Education	Inquiry into the academic, vocational, or professional education of an applicant and public and private schools attended	
Experience	Inquiry into work experience Inquiry into countries applicant has visited	
Arrests	Have you ever been convicted of a crime? Are there any felony charges pending against you?	Inquiry regarding arrests that did not result in conviction (except for law enforcement agencies)
Relatives	Names of applicant's relatives already employed by this company	Address of any relative of applicant, other than address (within the United States) of applicant's father and mother, husband or wife, and minor dependent children
Notice in case of emergency	Name and address of person to be notified in case of accident or emergency	Name and address of nearest relative to be notified in case of accident or emergency
Organizations	Inquiry into the organizations of which an applicant is a member, excluding organizations the name or character of which indicates the race, color, religion, national origin, or ancestry of its members	List all clubs, societies, and lodges to which the applicant belongs
Personal finance	None	Inquiries about financial problems, such as garnishment or bankruptcy

TIP

Always ask first. If you plan to investigate an applicant's background, get a signed consent form. You'll need that form to reassure schools and former employers that it's legally safe for them to give you information about the applicant. You can ask the applicant to sign the consent form at the same time as the application, or you can wait until the job interview. (See Chapter 6, "Doing Background Checks," for a suggested form.)

Sample Application Form

Below is a sample application form you can use or adapt for your own purposes.

Job Application

For [Name of Position]

Name: _____

Address: _____

_____

Telephone number: _____

Social Security Number: _____

Are you legally entitled to work in the United States? ___ Yes ___ No

Are you 18 years of age or older? ___ Yes ___ No

If not, please give your date of birth: _____

EDUCATION

High School

Name of school: _____

Location: _____

Number of years attended: _____

Did you graduate? ___ Yes ___ No

Date of graduation: _____

Trade School

Name of school: _____

Location: _____

Number of years attended: _____

Did you graduate? ___ Yes ___ No

Date of graduation: _____

College

Name of school: _____

Location: _____

Number of years attended: _____

Did you graduate? ____ Yes ____ No

Date of graduation: _____

What degree did you earn? _____

Graduate

Name of school: _____

Location: _____

Number of years attended: _____

Did you graduate? ____ Yes ____ No

Date of graduation: _____

What degree did you earn? _____

EMPLOYMENT HISTORY

Beginning with your most recent employment, please give the following information:

Employer: _____

Address: _____

_____

Job title: _____

Duties: _____

Dates of employment: _____

Salary: _____

Supervisor: _____

Telephone number: _____

Email address: _____

Reason for leaving, if not still employed: _____

_____

If still employed, can we contact this employer? ____ Yes ____ No

Employer: _____

Address: _____

_____

Job title: _____

Duties: _____

Dates of employment: _____

Salary: _____

Supervisor: _____

Telephone number: _____

Email address: _____

Reason for leaving: _____

_____

Employer: _____

Address: _____

_____

Job title: _____

Duties: _____

Dates of employment: _____

Salary: _____

Supervisor: _____

Telephone number: _____

Email address: _____

Reason for leaving: _____

PERSONAL REFERENCES

Please provide the names of two references who are not present or former employers and are not related to you.

Reference

Name: _____

Address: _____

_____

Telephone number: _____

Relationship: _____

Reference

Name: _____

Address: _____

_____

Telephone number: _____

Relationship: _____

ADDITIONAL QUALIFICATIONS

Please describe any other training, education, skills, or achievements that you feel should be considered. _____

_____

_____

_____

I understand that if I am hired, my employment will be "at-will." My employment may be terminated—or I may resign—at any time, with or without cause.

I have carefully completed this application form, and I verify that all the information that I have provided is accurate.

Date application completed: _____

Applicant's signature: _____

Distributing Application Forms

When an applicant inquires about the job, you can personally hand over an application form, or deliver it by fax, postal mail or email. If your business has a website, you can make the form available online.

Finding Potential Employees

There are certainly many qualified people who need the money and experience you're offering and who would be eager to work for you—if only they knew you had a job open. As described below, there are several tried and true ways for you to reach them.

Personal Recommendations

This is an amazingly simple, no-cost way to find a good worker. Just tell the people you know best that you're looking to hire someone. Explain the nature of your business if they don't already know it and describe the kind of employee you're hoping to hire.

Most people relish the idea of being matchmakers—helping out two people with one stroke. Even if you're not a social butterfly and your business network is relatively small, you may hit pay dirt. Relatives, of course, are a convenient source, as are friends. But also consider telling customers, clients, and suppliers that you're looking for someone to hire; any one of these people may have a relative or friend or colleague with the qualities you seek.

People in the same line of work as you may also know of good potential candidates. You might run into such contacts at a trade show, or a meeting of a special interest group, and consider checking a blog or two if there is not a ready community of similar businesses nearby. You can gain from even more casual connections, such as acquaintances you see from time to time at your book club, or your child's soccer game, or those who sing with you in a choir. All of them may be able to send helpful leads your way. In one case, a solo business owner told his barber he was looking to hire an employee. The barber let another customer know about the opening—and a match was made. The grateful business owner gave the barber a $100 tip.

Advertisements

It's relatively inexpensive to place ads. The Help Wanted section of your local newspaper is a logical starting point.

But don't overlook other places to advertise that also may be inexpensive or even free. For example, a local or regional newsletter may accept advertising, as do many professional and business publications. And don't ignore old-fashioned bulletin boards. The one at your nearby community center, health club, or supermarket may serve your purpose perfectly.

Advertising 101

If you've taken time to put together a solid job description, you've already done 90% of the work of writing a Help Wanted ad. A well-conceived summary gives you most of what you need for your ad.

Make sure your ad is written in plain English and describes the core duties of the job. Your ad should be concise because extra words are likely to cost you more. Luckily, an ad doesn't need full sentences. Short phrases can do the trick. Pay close attention to the wording, however, so your ad doesn't violate antidiscrimination standards. (Chapter 2, "Follow Anti-Discrimination Guidelines," explains how to avoid discrimination claims in a job description. Observe the same rules in your ad.)

A Help Wanted ad for an office assistant might look like this:

__Office Assistant__ for busy real estate appraiser. Thirty flexible hours a week. Job includes scheduling appraisals, helping to gather data, assembling appraisal reports, filing, and billing. Minimum two years of college required. Bookkeeping experience a plus. Competitive salary. Call 555-5555.

Internet Resources

A slew of websites let you post job openings. The list of such sites is changing and growing daily, so to find a site that's appropriate for you, you'll need to do some investigating.

Using a search engine, enter the phrase "job opportunities." This will bring up numerous sites potential employees frequent. Find out how to get listed on sites that seem promising. An industry-specific site on which people looking for a job can post their résumés can be a gold mine.

Employment Agencies

After receiving a job description, an employment agency will find and screen candidates for you. The agency typically will conduct interviews and check references, and—where appropriate—do background checks, credit checks, and testing. You'll then be given the opportunity to interview candidates who seem to meet your needs.

If you hire a person that the agency has sent you, you'll pay a fee based on the employee's first year's earnings. The fees are usually based on a sliding scale and are set by state law. In Michigan, for example, for an employee who will earn less than $10,000 a year, you would pay 10% of the first year's earnings; for an employee who will earn $28,000 or more, you would pay 30%. Read the agency's contract carefully so you know your exact obligations. The fee is due when you hire the employee, but you may be able to negotiate an installment payment plan if needed.

> **TIP**
>
> **Hiring a temp may be another option.** An employment agency may let you start out using an employee as a temporary worker. Then, if things work out, you can change over to an employment arrangement. A worker who qualifies as a temp is the agency's employee and the agency takes care of payroll and the employer's share of payroll taxes. Of course, the agency factors all of this plus a mark-up into the amount you pay for the temp's services. Once the worker becomes your employee, you then become

responsible for payroll and the associated taxes. If the temp has worked for a certain period—say, 520 hours or 90 days—you won't owe the agency a fee if you do hire the person, as the agency has earned its profit during the temp period.

High Schools and Colleges

Check at the high schools in your area, as well as any nearby community colleges and four-year colleges to see whether they have a program or policy of informing students and graduates about local job openings. What these applicants lack in experience may be offset by the fact they're likely to be eager and trainable—and some of them may have already acquired some knowledge and skills specific to your type of business.

Unemployment Offices

Your state's unemployment office almost certainly helps find work for people who've gotten bumped when a company downsized. Many of these workers have a wealth of experience, and one of them may be perfect for your needs.

For contact information, go to www.servicelocator.org/OWSLinks.asp.

Registering as an Employer

As you get ready to hire your first employee, there's another step you'll need to take in addition to preparing a job description and a job application: You'll need to register with the IRS if you haven't already done so, and perhaps register with your state government as well. If you deal with this detail early on, you won't have to play catch-up after your employee is on board. The process is simple.

Getting an Employer Identification Number

The IRS assigns a nine-digit Employer Identification Number, or EIN, to a business to identify and track the business on tax forms. If you have not already obtained an EIN, do so before you hire your first employee.

You'll need an EIN to deposit the income tax you withhold from your employee's paychecks, and the employer's and employee's shares of Social Security and Medicare taxes. (See Chapters 10, 11, and 12 for details on federal employment taxes and tax returns.) Getting an EIN is easy and quick, using one of two recommended methods described here.

Applying online. Go to www.irs.gov/businesses and click on "Starting a Business." Then click on the link to EINs, and from there go to "Apply for an EIN Online." You'll answer a series of questions and get your EIN immediately. You can then download, save, and print your confirmation notice.

> ⓘ **CAUTION**
>
> **Special rules may apply if you have a single-member LLC.** If you have a single-member LLC and will have an employee within the next 12 months, you'll need two EINs. One is assigned to you as the sole owner, and one is assigned to the LLC. If you don't already have an EIN for yourself, you cannot use the online application system. Instead, follow the instructions below for applying over the phone.

Applying over the phone. First, complete a hard copy version of IRS Form SS-4, *Application for Employer Identification,* available at www.irs. gov. Then call the IRS at 800-829-4933 between 7 a.m. and 10 p.m. You can read the information to the IRS representative, who will give you your EIN. Write the number on the upper right-hand corner of the form. Sign and date the form, and keep it for your records. You'll receive confirmation of your EIN by mail. While on the phone, the IRS representative may ask you to fax or mail a copy of the form to the IRS office.

You can also apply by completing Form SS-4 and mailing or faxing it to the IRS, but the online and phone methods are far more efficient.

> **TIP**
>
> **Hurry up and wait.** Whichever method you use, apply as soon as possible. It can take up to two weeks before your EIN becomes part of the government's permanent records.

Common Mistakes in Applying for and Using an Employer Identification Number

The IRS and experienced tax practitioners say that employers, in applying for and using an EIN, commonly make these mistakes:

- Not entering the full and correct legal name of the entity that is applying.
- Entering a trade name or "doing business as" on Line 1 instead of the legal name of the applicant.
- Using their EIN instead of their Social Security number on nonbusiness tax returns.
- Omitting their Social Security number on Form SS-4.
- Having someone other than an owner or principal officer sign the form when applying for an EIN.
- Signing in a color other than black or blue—which can be a problem for copiers, fax machines, and scanners.

For help in correcting these and other mistakes, contact the government's EIN specialists at 800-829-4933.

State Registration

In addition to the federal tax responsibilities that come with running a business that has an employee, you may also have employment tax obligations to your state government. You may, for example, need to withhold state income taxes on your employee's salary, and to pay your state's unemployment tax.

Your state may use the federal EIN number for one or more state employment taxes, but you must check to make sure. You may find that your federal EIN will work for income tax withholdings, but not for state unemployment taxes. If your business is in California, for example, you must register with the Employment Development Department, or EDD, and obtain an EDD account number. On the California registration form, you'll need to include information not required on IRS Form SS-4, including the names, Social Security numbers, and driver's license numbers of individual owners, partners, corporate officers, or LLC members.

RESOURCE

Contact your state revenue department and unemployment agency to learn about their registration procedures for employment taxes. For contact information for your state's revenue department, go to www .toolkit.cch.com/text/P07_1278.asp, and click on your state on the map. For contact information on your state's unemployment agency, go to www.toolkit.cch.com/text/P07_1294.asp, where you'll also find a map for specifics.

Screening Applicants
and Making a Job Offer

he preceding chapter gave advice and practical suggestions about how to find an interested and qualified candidate to hire as your employee. This one concentrates on what to do once you've found one or more promising prospects.

After narrowing in on a few top potential candidates as part of the initial screening process, you may want to contact their former employers for more information. For some jobs, you may also want to perform a more thorough background check. This might include verifying educational credentials, learning the applicant's driving history, or checking to see if an applicant has a criminal record. And occasionally, you may also want to test an applicant. This chapter explains how to do background checks and describes the legal limits on them.

You'll certainly want to learn more about each potential employee through a face-to-face interview. This chapter offers advice on how to prepare for and conduct interviews to make that process go smoothly. It helps you come up with productive questions to ask—and explains how to avoid common interview mistakes that might lead to legal trouble.

Preparing for an Interview

After you have received job applications from potential employees, the next logical step is to interview the ones who look good on paper. A good interview is a two-way street: The applicant learns about the job, and you learn about the applicant. Conducting a productive interview isn't complicated, but it's also not as intuitive as you may think. To help ensure a successful interview, it is wise to spend a bit of time preparing, almost as if you were interviewing yourself for the position.

Start with the things you want to tell the applicant—or at least be ready to talk about if you are asked about them:

- **Job duties.** What will a typical workday look like? What nonroutine or unexpected duties might the employee face? Will the employee be dealing with other people—such as customers, clients, or suppliers?
- **Workplace conditions.** Where will the employee be working? What equipment will you be providing?

- **Parking and transportation.** Will the employee need to use a personal car as part of the job? Is there parking nearby? What public transportation is available?

- **Travel.** Will the employee need to travel out of town? To do what? How often will there be travel assignments? Will this involve staying overnight?

- **Attire.** Are there special requirements for what the employee should wear to work? Will you provide a uniform, or a clothing allowance?

- **Schedule.** What are normal working hours? Will the employee be expected to work overtime or on holidays or weekends? If so, how often?

- **Salary.** How much will you pay? How often will the employee receive a paycheck?

- **Benefits.** Do you offer paid time off for vacations? Do you offer paid sick days? Do you offer health or dental insurance?

- **Training.** Will you be giving the employee special training? What other opportunities will the employee have to acquire new skills, such as by attending conferences and seminars?

Be prepared to give the applicant a clear picture of what to expect if hired. If you leave out some crucial detail, an applicant who later becomes an employee may be surprised and upset and feel duped. This can affect job performance—and the employee may even quit. So paint a full and honest picture, and don't create expectations you won't be able to satisfy.

Then shift gears and think about the part of the interview in which you concentrate on learning more about the applicant. During the actual interview—and any follow-up—you'll need to determine whether or not the applicant meets or exceeds the basic job requirements, such as education level and experience. This part of the screening process should be relatively straightforward.

It's much more challenging to decide on the intangible personal qualities you're seeking in an employee. It pays to think this through before you start an interview so that you can probe for relevant information more effectively.

For example, if the job involves dealing with customers or clients every day, you will likely want an employee who has an amiable personality and the ability to get along well with a wide range of people. You may also be looking for someone who is well groomed.

By contrast, if the employee won't be dealing much with others, and in fact will be working alone much of the time, you may want to look for signs that the applicant is a self-starter who can work without close supervision. People skills and personal appearance may be much less important for such positions.

Depending on the job, other desirable attributes may include:

• creativity

• maturity—not to be confused with age

• energy, and

• self-confidence.

Probing Areas of Concern

By the interview stage, the applicant probably has given you a résumé or a completed application form. (See Chapter 5 for details on job applications.) Take time to study these documents, as they may raise issues that you'd like to get clarified.

For example, the applicant may have omitted contact information about his or her last employer. Or there may be mysterious gaps in the applicant's work history. Maybe the applicant has not held a job for longer than three months. Or perhaps a job title appears to be vague or inflated. Are these matters significant? It's hard to know. There may be perfectly valid explanations. Then again, these may be signs of underlying problems.

If your antennae are alerted to any potential problems when you peruse a résumé or application, be prepared to explore them when you interview the applicant.

Taking Legal Precautions

As discussed in Chapter 2, "Avoiding Legal Pitfalls," there are a number of potential legal stumbling blocks to keep in mind during the hiring process—and some are especially important to bear in mind when conducting interviews.

Preserve Employment at-Will

The doctrine of employment at will means that you can fire an employee at any time as long as it's for not an illegal reason, such as for reporting a safety violation, for example. During an interview, be careful not to compromise your freedom to fire by promising or even implying job security. If you hire and then fire the applicant, you don't want him or her to sue you, claiming that you promised there would be a good reason for a firing, and that there was none.

Don't Exaggerate

Be careful not to inflate your business's long-term prospects—especially if the applicant will be giving up other attractive job opportunities to come work for you. If you paint too rosy a picture and your business doesn't grow or doesn't deliver the bonuses as expected, you may wind up with a disgruntled employee. Worse yet, you may have to defend against a legal claim based on alleged misrepresentation or breach of contract.

Avoid Discriminating

Steer clear of questions that relate to age, race, religion, marital status, citizenship, or national origin. (Look again at the chart in Chapter 5, "Preemployment Inquiries," for specific guidance on question you can and cannot ask.)

In interviewing, these restrictions sometimes arise in unexpected ways. For example, do not ask an applicant: "When did you graduate from high school?" Such a question is almost the same as asking the person's age, which is a clearly illegal probe.

And bear in mind that child care and parental care can also be sensitive interview topics. A growing number of laws protect employees from being discriminated against because of family responsibilities. But if you need to probe for some job-related information that may tangentially touch on such issues, the safest way to proceed from a legal standpoint is to explain what the job requires, and then ask if this will be a problem. For example: "During crunches at the end of each month, you may be asked to work late or on weekends. Will this be a problem for you?"

Finally, be especially careful with applicants with disabilities. Sometimes an applicant's disability is obvious. Other times the applicant may disclose the fact of a physical or mental disability. The important thing is to focus on the applicant's abilities, not disabilities. About the only safe question is: "Can you perform the job with or without an accommodation?" The term "accommodation" is legal jargon for some reasonable step you might take to make it possible for the person to do the job. (Special rules also apply if you're thinking of requiring a medical exam—a topic covered below. Do not discuss medical testing during an interview).

TIP

Consider prescreening applicants by phone. Doing some advance screening by telephone may be an essential timesaver, especially if there are a lot of applicants. As an additional benefit, this can also be a useful way to gauge an applicant's phone demeanor, if that's an important part of the job.

Conducting the Interview

This section contains practical pointers for conducting effective job interviews, with particular attention to potential legal trouble spots.

If you're interviewing several candidates, keep the interviews as similar as possible so that you have a better basis for comparison. It helps to write down your questions in advance so you can seek the same information from each candidate. You'll need to deviate from your script, of course, with follow-up questions and requests for clarification of information in an application form or résumé. Reserve ample time for the interview to assure that neither you nor the applicant will feel rushed.

TIP

Show and tell may be appropriate. It may be helpful to ask applicants to bring in samples of past similar work, especially if the job requires creativity. For example, if you're hiring someone to assist you in your catering business, you might ask applicants to bring in samples of their signature dishes. For an advertising job, you might request writing or art samples. For a space planning job, you can ask to see layouts and photos. An applicant's past performance can be a good indicator of what you can expect if you hire that person.

Start by briefly explaining what the job entails. This is easy to do if you've prepared a job description. (See Chapter 5, "Job Descriptions," for details). But even without a written description, you should be able to spell out the job duties and perhaps even describe what a typical day on the job will look like. You can then ask: "Any questions so far?" This encourages the applicant to speak up, gives you the chance you may need to regroup, and helps ensure that you haven't omitted any information that may be important to clarify.

Next, you might go through the candidate's application form to fill in any gaps and to gain a better idea of individual skills and workplace experience. If the job requires specialized skills, you might ask questions that focus on them. If you're looking for someone to assist you in your small catering business, for example, you might ask about the applicant's knowledge of or experience in preparing salads or appetizers. Or for further insights into the applicant's culinary skills, you might ask about favorite recipes.

> **TIP**
>
> **Listen closely.** During an interview, a job applicant's words can open the door to useful follow-up questions. Feel free to veer away from your prepared list of questions and let the applicant's answers lead you into some unanticipated areas. You can always return to preplanned questions when the side trip is over.

You can then ask some additional open-ended questions to help get a handle on the applicant's personality. For example:

- "What did you like best about your last job?"
- "What did you find most frustrating?"
- "What was your favorite class in school?"
- "How do you feel about making sales pitches to customers?"
- "What appeals to you most about the job opening here?"
- "What's the greatest asset you'd bring to the job?"

Next, if there are specific aspects of the job you need to emphasize, you can ask some pointed questions:

- "If I hire you, you'll need to work at least one Sunday a month. Will that be a problem?"
- "The person I hire will occasionally need to run the shop all alone. Would you be okay with that?"
- "The job requires using a computer spreadsheet for recording rent payments. Are you willing to become proficient using spreadsheet software?"

Then you can begin to wind up the interview. Ask again if the applicant has any additional questions or concerns. Then ask a few wrap-up questions, such as:

- "Have I covered everything for you?"
- "Do you still want to be considered for this job?"
- "If you're chosen for the job, when could you start?"

These questions can help you weed out weak candidates—those who are not enthusiastically interested in becoming your employee, but just need a job.

Before the interview is over, if you haven't already done so, you can ask the applicant to sign a consent form to allow you to seek information from schools, past employers, and credit agencies. (See "Consent for Release of Employment Information," below.)

TIP

Consider testing the applicant's skills. If, for example, you're looking to hire someone who will compose and type letters, you might decide to give a typing test. For some types of jobs, you might also decide to give a spelling or grammar test. If you're hiring someone to use power tools in your shop, you may want to run through a hands-on test to make sure the applicant really is qualified.

RESOURCE

To learn more about conducting an effective interview, see *96 Great Interview Questions to Ask Before You Hire,* by Paul Falcone (AMACOM), and *Recruiting, Interviewing, Selecting & Orienting New Employees,* by Diane Arthur (AMACOM).

Testing Applicants Can Get Tricky

In hiring your first employee, it's unlikely that you'll feel a need to administer many tests other than those aimed at evaluating particular skills. That's good, because as described below, a slew of federal and state laws restrict what you are allowed to do.

- **Psychological tests.** A number of multiple-choice tests are available that purport to assess an applicant's abilities or personality. But these tests may really only reveal an applicant's ability to take tests—and they may discriminate against members of some minority groups. In addition, personality tests may break the law by invading an applicant's privacy or discriminating against someone with a psychological disability. Internet services that offer to screen applicants based on their personality traits are likely to be a waste of money, and might also get you in legal trouble for trampling on protected rights.

- **Honesty tests.** Unless your first employee will be providing armored car, alarm, or guard services or will be manufacturing, distributing, or dispensing pharmaceuticals, federal law prohibits requiring lie detector or polygraph tests. Even then, a strict law—the Employee Polygraph Protection Act—sets out many strictures on the form and procedures for such testing. Written honesty tests can also pose problems. They may invade an applicant's privacy or violate antidiscrimination laws.

- **Medical tests.** You can't require an applicant to be medically tested. You can, however, make a job offer conditional on the applicant passing a medical exam, so timing is everything. You may want an applicant to take a medical exam if the job is physically strenuous, or requires using dangerous equipment. If you do ask for a medical exam, you should apply the requirement to all job offers—not just offers to people who have or may have a disability. (See Chapter 8, "Employee Files," for rules on storing medical information.)

- **Drug tests.** You can insist on a drugfree workplace. This may be important to you—especially if the job calls for driving a car or truck or operating power equipment. In general, you can test applicants if:
  - they know it is part of the screening process
  - you have actually offered the job
  - you test all applicants who are offered a job, and
  - the test is conducted by a state-certified lab.

If you intend to do any testing other than skills testing, it is probably wise to consult a lawyer first.

Checking References

If an applicant seems promising during a personal interview, it's reasonable to contact any former employers afterward to plumb for more information. Be aware, however, that a former employer may not give you a full and accurate report.

In fact, the employer may be reluctant to say anything negative, and may even be unwilling to say much at all—including positive comments—preferring instead to simply verify the dates of employment. This reluctance may be traced to a recent rash of lawsuits by former employees who sued their past employers, claiming they gave negative and damaging reports about them that hurt their reputations in the working world. But the hesitance about telling the truth is overkill, really, since laws in most states protect former employers who stick to the facts and act in good faith in giving information to a prospective new employer.

Still, many former employers are willing to speak candidly with you, so contacting them won't always be a wasted effort. But before disclosing any information, many former employers will want to be assured that the employee has consented to the contact.

To secure permission, you can ask the applicant to sign a consent form such as the one below. You can then mail or fax the form to former employers, explaining that you will be phoning them to learn more about the applicant. When you do make those calls, ask not only to verify facts but also about the applicant's competence, attitude, ability to work with people, attendance record, and anything else that may help you decide whether to hire the person.

Sample Consent Form

Consent for Release of Employment Information

I have applied for employment at Arbor Rentals, LLC. I authorize and request each of my former employers to release to Arbor Rentals, LLC all information concerning my former employment and the circumstances of my leaving that employment.

Name: _____

Social Security Number: _____

Address: _____

Signature: _____

TIP

Seek references who are not former employers. People who know an applicant but have not acted as his or her employer are likely to be more talkative. While it's true that the applicant will have hand-picked these references, they may reveal information about the applicant's character and accomplishments that the applicant may be too modest to mention.

Doing Background Checks

In most cases, information you get while speaking with an applicant's former employers and other references will be sufficient for you to get a picture of likely strengths and weaknesses as a worker.

But occasionally, you may want to dig deeper by conducting a background check. You may, for example, want to confirm an applicant's educational credentials that are required for the job, or see whether the applicant has had financial problems if the job involves handling money. Or perhaps something a former employer said raises questions for you that bear more probing.

Laws protecting individual privacy may sometimes limit the scope of your inquiries. In deciding whether to conduct a background check, be guided by your intuition and the nature of the job, and be sure you have a good business reason for doing the checking. This section explains some of the specific legal constraints on doing such checking.

> ⓘ **CAUTION**
>
> **Be wary of computerized background checks.** You may be tempted by online ads from companies promising to do various types of background checks on job applicants. While these services may appear to save you time and effort, they can be expensive, and they may not be as complete and accurate as you'd like—especially if the company doesn't require the applicant's written consent. Without that consent, the company isn't tapping into key information, or is using underhanded methods. Such operators are best avoided.

Educational Records

For some jobs, you may want to verify whether an applicant has the educational credentials claimed, which may include completing high school, college, or other educational or training institution. For example, if you're hiring someone to edit manuscripts, you may want to see a college transcript to confirm that an applicant did indeed graduate as an English major as represented on a résumé.

This is confidential information, so you'll need the applicant's consent before contacting the school for verification. But even having the applicant's consent won't guarantee that the school will send you the applicant's records, as some schools will only send this information to the student. Call the school to learn its policy. If it follows a student-only policy, ask the applicant to obtain the records for you. Be aware, too, that some schools provide their own consent forms.

Ask school administrators where you should get the consent form. Then mail it—or fax it, if that is acceptable—along with a cover letter requesting the information you seek. It might be confirmation of graduation, dates of attendance, or a transcript of courses and grades.

Sample Consent Form

Consent for Release of Educational Records

I have applied for employment at Greenway Graphics, Inc. I authorize and request the following educational institutions to release to Greenway Graphics a copy of my transcripts and other educational records:

Name: _____

Social Security Number: _____

Address: _____

Signature: _____

TIP

Some credentials are publicly available. If an applicant claims to have a state license or certificate—verifying the ability to work as a barber, for example, or a home remodeler—you can generally verify this through a call to the licensing or certifying agency. Often, this information is also available online. Where information is public, you don't need the applicant's written consent to look at it. You may also be able to get information about complaints or disciplinary action concerning a license or certificate, either by calling the licensing agency or visiting its website.

Credit Reports

If a job requires an employee to handle large amounts of cash, it makes sense to get a credit report, as someone with excessive debt may have sticky fingers. A credit report will tell you how much debt the applicant has, and whether he or she is paying bills on time. But there are rigid legal constraints about getting such information. And because it's such a hassle to deal with credit reports, you may decide it's not worth it except in rare situations.

A federal law—the Fair Credit Reporting Act—requires you to notify the applicant in writing that you're going to order a credit report, and also requires you to get the applicant's written consent before you order it.

When you order a credit report, the reporting agency will probably want to see a copy of the applicant's consent. But whether or not that is so, be sure to keep the original or a copy in case the applicant later claims that you lacked permission to obtain the report.

Sample Consent Form

Consent for Release of Credit Reports

I have applied for employment at Aberdeen Accounting. I authorize and request the following credit reporting agencies to release my credit report to Aberdeen:

Name: _____

Social Security Number: _____

Address: _____

Signature: _____

You can order a credit report from a local credit bureau, or from one of the three national companies: Equifax (www.equifax.com), Experian (www.experian.com), or TransUnion (www.transunion.com). Expect to pay about $10 for a credit report.

If You Don't Like What You See

If, based on the credit report, you decide not to hire a particular applicant, you must take definitive steps required by law.

You must give the applicant a copy of the credit report and a copy of *A Summary of Your Rights Under the Fair Credit Reporting Act.* This is a publication of the Federal Trade Commission (FTC). You can get it from the credit reporting company, or from the FTC at www.ftc.gov/bcp/conline/pubs/credit/fcrasummary.pdf.

Then, notify the applicant that you're not going to hire him or her. You can do this orally, in writing, by email, or by fax. Your notice must:

- give the name, address, and phone number of the company that supplied the report
- state that the company didn't make the decision not to hire the applicant, and
- inform the applicant of the right to dispute the accuracy or the completeness of the report.

You must also notify the applicant of the right to request an additional free credit report from the credit reporting company.

Criminal History

If the employee will be working with children or entering the homes of customers or clients, it's reasonable to check on whether he or she has a criminal history.

And you may need a criminal history check to help ensure your own legal safety. For example, if you hire some who's been convicted of a sexual offense or a violent crime and you haven't done a reasonable check, and the employee commits a similar crime while on the job, the victim or victim's family may sue you for allowing the danger to occur.

You may also want to check an applicant's criminal history if the job involves dealing with large sums of cash or handling valuable property.

Laws vary from state to state on what information you can properly consider. In many states, for example, you can only consider convictions and not arrests. And in some of those states, the crime must be relevant to the job.

> **CAUTION**
>
> **Criminal record checks may be mandatory.** Some states require a criminal record search if your employee will be dealing with vulnerable people, such as children and elderly adults. A search might be required in your state, for example, if your employee will be involved in child care or home health care. Your local police department or your state's attorney general's office should be able to tell you if a criminal record check is mandatory in your state. But even if it isn't, you should consider doing such a check if your employee will be in a position to harm vulnerable people.

State Laws on Employee Arrest and Conviction Records

The following chart summarizes state laws and regulations on whether an employer can get access to an employee's or prospective employee's past arrests or convictions. It includes citations to statutes and agency websites, as available.

Many states allow or require private sector employers to run background checks on workers, particularly in fields like child care, elder care, home health care, private schools, private security, and the investment industry. Criminal background checks usually consist of sending the applicant's name (and sometimes fingerprints) to the state police or to the FBI. State law may forbid hiring people with certain kinds of prior convictions, depending on the kind of job or license involved.

Federal law allows the states to establish procedures for requesting a nationwide background check to find out if a person has been "convicted of a crime that bears upon the [person's] fitness to have responsibility for the safety and well-being of children, the elderly, or individuals with disabilities." (42 U.S.C.A. § 5119a(a)(1).)

If your state isn't listed in this chart, then it doesn't have a *general statute* on whether private sector employers can find out about arrests or convictions. There might be a law about your particular industry, though.

It's always a good idea to consult your state's nondiscrimination enforcement agency or labor department to see what kinds of questions you can ask. The agency guidelines are designed to help employers comply with state and federal law. For further information, contact your state's agency.

Alaska

Agency guidelines for preemployment inquiries: Alaska Department of Labor and Workforce Development, Alaska Employer Handbook, "Pre-Employment Questioning," at www.labor.state.ak.us/employer/aeh.pdf.

Arizona

Ariz. Rev. Stat. § 13-904(E)

Rights of employees and applicants: Unless the offense has a reasonable relationship to the occupation, an occupational license may not be denied solely on the basis of a felony or misdemeanor conviction.

California

Cal. Lab. Code § 432.7

Rules for employers:

- **Arrest records.** May not ask about an arrest that did not lead to conviction; may not ask about pretrial or posttrial diversion program. May ask about arrest if prospective employee is awaiting trial.
- **Convictions.** May ask about conviction even if no sentence is imposed.

Agency guidelines for preemployment inquiries: Department of Fair Employment and Housing, "Pre-Employment Inquiry Guidelines," DFEH-161 at www.dfeh.ca.gov/Publications/publications.aspx?showPub=9.

Colorado

Colo. Rev. Stat. §§ 24-72-308(b)(II)(f)(I), 8-3-108(m)

Rules for employers: May not inquire about arrest for civil or military disobedience unless it resulted in conviction.

Rights of employees and applicants: May not be required to disclose any information in

State Laws on Employee Arrest and Conviction Records (cont'd)

a sealed record; may answer questions about arrests or convictions as though they had not occurred.

Agency guidelines for preemployment inquiries: Colorado Civil Rights Division, "Preventing Job Discrimination," at www. dora.state.co.us/civil-rights/Publications/ JobDiscrim2001.pdf.

Connecticut

Conn. Gen. Stat. Ann. §§ 46a-79, 46a-80, 31-51i

Rules for employers: State policy encourages hiring qualified applicants with criminal records. If an employment application form contains any question concerning criminal history, it must include a notice in clear and conspicuous language that (1) the applicant is not required to disclose the existence of any arrest, criminal charge, or conviction, the records of which have been erased; (2) defining what criminal records are subject to erasure; and (3) any person whose criminal records have been erased will be treated as if never arrested and my swear so under oath. Employer may not disclose information about a job applicant's criminal history except to members of the personnel department or, if there is no personnel department, person(s) in charge of hiring or conducting the interview.

Rights of employees and applicants: May not be asked to disclose information about a criminal record that has been erased; may answer any question as though arrest or conviction never took place. May not be discriminated against in hiring or continued employment on the basis of an erased criminal record. If conviction of a crime has been used as a basis to reject an applicant,

the rejection must be in writing and specifically state the evidence presented and the reason for rejection.

Special situations: Each consumer reporting agency that issues a consumer report used or expected to be used for employment purposes and that includes in such report criminal matters of public record concerning the consumer shall provide the consumer who is the subject of the consumer report (1) notice that the consumer reporting agency is reporting criminal matters of public record, and (2) the name and address of the person to whom such consumer report is being issued.

Delaware

Del. Code Ann. tit. 11, § 4374(e)

Rights of employees and applicants: Do not have to disclose an arrest or conviction record that has been expunged.

Florida

Fla. Stat. Ann. § 112.011

Rights of employees and applicants: May not be disqualified to practice or pursue any occupation or profession that requires a license, permit, or certificate because of a prior conviction, unless it was for a felony or first-degree misdemeanor and is directly related to the specific line of work.

Georgia

Ga. Code Ann. §§ 35-3-34, 42-8-62, 42-8-63

Rules for employers: In order to obtain a criminal record from the state Crime Information Center, employer must supply the individual's fingerprints or signed consent. If an adverse employment decision

State Laws on Employee Arrest and Conviction Records (cont'd)

is made on the basis of the record, employer must disclose all information in the record to the employee or applicant and tell how it affected the decision.

Rights of employees and applicants: Probation for a first offense is not a conviction; may not be disqualified for employment once probation is completed.

Hawaii

Haw. Rev. Stat. §§ 378-2, 378-2.5, 831-3.2

Rules for employers:

- **Arrest records.** It is a violation of law for any employer to refuse to hire, to discharge, or to discriminate in terms of compensation, conditions, or privileges of employment because of a person's arrest or court record.
- **Convictions.** May inquire into a conviction only after making a conditional offer of employment, provided it has a rational relation to job. May not examine any convictions over 10 years old.

Rights of employees and applicants: If an arrest or conviction has been expunged, may state that no record exists and may respond to questions as a person with no record would respond.

Agency guidelines for preemployment inquiries: Hawaii Civil Rights Commission, "What is Employment Discrimination?" at www.hawaii.gov/labor/hcrc/pdf/HCRCemploymdiscrim.pdf.

Idaho

Agency guidelines for preemployment inquiries: Idaho Human Rights Commission, "Conducting a Lawful Employment Interview," at http://cl.idaho.gov/lawintvw3.pdf.

Illinois

775 Ill. Comp. Stat. § 5/2-103

Rules for employers: It is a civil rights violation to ask about an arrest or criminal history record that has been expunged or sealed, or to use the fact of an arrest or criminal history record as a basis for refusing to hire or to renew employment. Law does not prohibit employer from using other means to find out if person actually engaged in conduct for which he was arrested.

Kansas

Kan. Stat. Ann. §§ 22-4710

Rules for employers: Cannot require an employee to inspect or challenge a criminal record in order to obtain a copy of the record, but may require an applicant to sign a release to allow employer to obtain record to determine fitness for employment. Employers can require access to criminal records for specific businesses.

Agency guidelines for preemployment inquiries: Kansas Human Rights Commission, "Guidelines on Equal Employment Practices: Preventing Discrimination in Hiring," at www.khrc.net/hiring.html.

State Laws on Employee Arrest and Conviction Records (cont'd)

Louisiana

La. Rev. Stat. Ann. § 37:2950

Rights of employees and applicants: Prior conviction cannot be used as a sole basis to deny employment or an occupational or professional license, unless conviction is for a felony and directly relates to the job or license being sought.

Special situations: Protection does not apply to medical, engineering and architecture, or funeral and embalming licenses, among others listed in the statute.

Maine

Me. Rev. Stat. Ann. tit. 5, § 5301

Rights of employees and applicants: A conviction is not an automatic bar to obtaining an occupational or professional license. Only convictions that directly relate to the profession or occupation, that include dishonesty or false statements, that are subject to imprisonment for more than one year, or that involve sexual misconduct on the part of a licensee may be considered.

Agency guidelines for preemployment inquiries: The Maine Human Rights Commission, "Pre-employment Inquiry Guide," at www.maine.gov/mhrc/publications/pre-employment_inquiry_guide.html, suggests that asking about arrests is an improper race-based question, but that it is okay to ask about a conviction if related to the job.

Maryland

Md. Ann. Code [Crim. Proc.], § 10-109; Md. Regs. Code 09.01.10.02

Rules for employers: May not inquire about any criminal charges that have been expunged. May not use a refusal to disclose information as sole basis for not hiring an applicant.

Rights of employees and applicants: Need not refer to or give any information about an expunged charge. A professional or occupational license may not be refused or revoked simply because of a conviction; agency must consider the nature of the crime and its relation to the occupation or profession, the conviction's relevance to the applicant's fitness and qualifications, when conviction occurred and other convictions, if any, and the applicant's behavior before and after conviction.

Agency guidelines for preemployment inquiries: The Office of Equal Opportunity and Program Equity, "Guidelines for Pre-Employment Inquiries Technical Assistance Guide," at www.dllr.state.md.us/oeope/preemp.htm.

Massachusetts

Mass. Gen. Laws ch. 151B, § 4; ch. 276, § 100A; Mass. Regs. Code tit. 804, § 3.02

Rules for employers: If job application has a question about prior arrests or convictions, it must include a formulated statement (that appears in the statute) that states that an applicant with a sealed record is entitled to answer, "No record."

- **Arrest records.** May not ask about arrests that did not result in conviction.
- **Convictions.** May not ask about first-time convictions for drunkenness, simple assault, speeding, minor traffic violations, or disturbing the peace; may not ask about misdemeanor convictions five or more years old.

State Laws on Employee Arrest and Conviction Records (cont'd)

Rights of employees and applicants: If criminal record is sealed, may answer, "No record" to any inquiry about past arrests or convictions.

Agency guidelines for preemployment inquiries: Massachusetts Commission Against Discrimination, "Fact Sheet: Discrimination on the Basis of Criminal Record," at www.mass.gov/mcad/crimrec. html.

Michigan

Mich. Comp. Laws § 37.2205a

Rules for employers: May not request information on any arrests or misdemeanor charges that did not result in conviction.

Rights of employees and applicants: Employees or applicants are not making a false statement if they fail to disclose information they have a civil right to withhold.

Agency guidelines for preemployment inquiries: Michigan Department of Civil Rights, "Pre-Employment Inquiry Guide," at www.michigan.gov/documents/pre-employment_inquery_guide_13019_7.pdf.

Minnesota

Minn. Stat. Ann. §§ 364.01 to 364.03

Rules for employers: State policy encourages the rehabilitation of criminal offenders; employment opportunity is considered essential to rehabilitation.

Rights of employees and applicants: No one can be disqualified from pursuing or practicing an occupation that requires a license, unless the crime directly relates to the occupation. Agency may consider the nature and seriousness of the crime and its relation to the applicant's fitness for the occupation. Even if the crime does relate to the occupation, a person who provides evidence of rehabilitation and present fitness cannot be disqualified.

Agency guidelines for preemployment inquiries: Minnesota Department of Human Rights, "Hiring, Job Interviews and the Minnesota Human Rights Act," at www.humanrights.state.mn.us/employer_hiring.html.

Missouri

Agency guidelines for preemployment inquiries: Commission on Human Rights, Missouri Department of Labor and Industrial Relations, "Pre-employment Inquiries," at www.dolir.mo.gov/hr/interview.htm.

Nebraska

Neb. Rev. Stat. § 29-3523

Rules for employers: After one year from date of arrest, may not obtain access to information regarding arrests if no charges are completed or pending.

Nevada

Nev. Rev. Stat. Ann. §§ 179.301, 179A.100(3)

Rules for employers: May obtain a prospective employee's criminal history record only if it includes convictions or a pending charge, including parole or probation.

Special situations: State Gaming Board may inquire into sealed records to see if conviction relates to gaming.

Agency guidelines for preemployment inquiries: Nevada Equal Rights Commission,

State Laws on Employee Arrest and Conviction Records (cont'd)

"Pre-Employment Inquiry Guide," at http://detr.state.nv.us/nerc/nerc_preemp.htm.

New Hampshire

N.H. Rev. Stat. Ann. § 651:5(X)(c)

Rules for employers: May ask about a previous criminal record only if question substantially follows this wording, "Have you ever been arrested for or convicted of a crime that has not been annulled by a court?"

- **Arrest records.** It is unlawful discrimination for an employer to ask about an arrest record, to have a job requirement that applicant have no arrest record, or to use information about arrest record to make a hiring decision, unless it is a business necessity. It is unlawful discrimination to ask about arrest record if it has the purpose or effect of discouraging applicants of a particular racial or national origin group.

New Jersey

N.J. Stat. Ann. §§ 5:5-34.1, 5:12-89 to 5:12-91, 32:23-86; N.J. Admin. Code tit. 13, §§ 59-1.2, 59-1.6

Rules for employers: May obtain information about convictions and pending arrests or charges to determine the subject's qualifications for employment. Employers must certify that they will provide sufficient time for applicant to challenge, correct, or complete record, and will not presume guilt for any pending charges or court actions.

Rights of employees and applicants: Applicant who is disqualified for employment based on criminal record must be given adequate notice and reasonable time to confirm or deny accuracy of information.

Special situations: There are specific rules for casino employees, longshoremen and related occupations, horse racing, and other gaming industry jobs.

New Mexico

Criminal Offender Employment Act, N.M. Stat. Ann. § 28-2-3

For a license, permit, or other authority to engage in any regulated trade, business, or profession, a regulating agency may consider convictions for felonies and for misdemeanors involving moral turpitude. Such convictions cannot be an automatic bar to authority to practice in the regulated field, however.

New York

N.Y. Correct. Law §§ 750 to 754; N.Y. Exec. Law § 296(16)

Rules for employers:
- **Arrest records**. It is unlawful discrimination to ask about any arrests or charges that did not result in conviction, unless they are currently pending.
- **Convictions.** Employers with 10 or more employees may not deny employment based on a conviction unless it relates directly to the job or would be an "unreasonable" risk to property or to public or individual safety.

Rights of employees and applicants: Upon request, applicant must be given, within 30 days, a written statement of the reasons why employment was denied.

Agency guidelines for preemployment inquiries: New York State Division of Human Rights, "Recommendations

State Laws on Employee Arrest and Conviction Records (cont'd)

on Employment Inquiries," at www.
dhr.state.ny.us/pdf/employment.
pdf#search=%22employment%20
inquiries%22.

North Dakota

N.D. Cent. Code § 12-60-16.6

Rules for employers: May obtain records
of convictions or of criminal charges (adults
only) occurring in the past three years,
provided the information has not been
purged or sealed.

**Agency guidelines for preemployment
inquiries:** North Dakota Department of
Labor, "Employment Applications and
Interviews," www.nd.gov/labor/publications/
docs/brochures/005.pdf.

Ohio

Ohio Rev. Code Ann. §§ 2151.357, 2953.33, 2953.55.

Rules for employers: May not inquire
into any sealed convictions or sealed bail
forfeitures, unless question has a direct and
substantial relation to job.

Rights of employees and applicants: May not
be asked about arrest records that are sealed;
may respond to inquiry as though arrest did not
occur.

Oklahoma

Okla. Stat. Ann. tit. 22, § 19(F)

Rules for employers: May not inquire into
any criminal record that has been expunged.

Rights of employees and applicants:
If record is expunged, may state that no
criminal action ever occurred. May not be
denied employment solely for refusing to
disclose sealed criminal record information.

Oregon

Or. Rev. Stat. §§ 181.555, 181.557, 181.560, 659A.030

Rules for employers: Before requesting
information, employer must notify employee
or applicant; when submitting request, must
tell State Police Department when and how
person was notified. May not discriminate
against an applicant or current employee
on the basis of an expunged juvenile record
unless there is a "bona fide occupational
qualification."

- **Arrest records.** May request information
  about arrest records less than one year
  old that have not resulted in acquittal or
  have not been dismissed.
- **Convictions.** May request information
  about conviction records.

Rights of employees and applicants:
Before State Police Department releases any
criminal record information, it must notify
employee or applicant and provide a copy of
all information that will be sent to employer.
Notice must include protections under
federal civil rights law and the procedure for
challenging information in the record. Record
may not be released until 14 days after notice
is sent.

Pennsylvania

18 Pa. Cons. Stat. Ann. § 9125

Rules for employers: May consider felony
and misdemeanor convictions only if they
directly relate to person's suitability for the
job.

Rights of employees and applicants: Must
be informed in writing if refusal to hire is
based on criminal record information.

State Laws on Employee Arrest and Conviction Records (cont'd)

Agency guidelines for preemployment inquiries: Pennsylvania Human Relations Commission, Pre-Employment Inquiries, at sites.state.pa.us/PA_Exec/PHRC/publications/literature/Pre-Employ%20 QandA%208x11%20READ.pdf.

Rhode Island

R.I. Gen. Laws §§ 12-1.3-4, 28-5-7(7)

Rules for employers:

- **Arrest records.** It is unlawful to include on an application form or to ask as part of an interview if the applicant has ever been arrested or charged with any crime.
- **Convictions.** May ask if applicant has been convicted of a crime.

Rights of employees and applicants: Do not have to disclose any conviction that has been expunged.

South Dakota

Agency guidelines for preemployment inquiries: South Dakota Division of Human Rights, "Pre-Employment Inquiry Guide," at www.state.sd.us/dol/boards/hr/preemplo. htm suggests that an employer shouldn't ask or check into arrests or convictions if they are not substantially related to the job.

Utah

Utah Admin. R. 606-2(V).

Rules for employers: Utah Labor Commission Antidiscrimination Rules, Rule R606-2. "Pre-Employment Inquiry Guide," at www.rules.utah.gov/publicat/code/r606/ r606-002.htm.

- **Arrest records.** It is not permissible to ask about arrests.

- **Convictions.** Asking about felony convictions is permitted but is not advisable unless related to job.

Vermont

Vt. Stat. Ann. tit. 20, § 2056c

Rules for employers: Only employers who provide care for children, the elderly, and the disabled or who run postsecondary schools with residential facilities may obtain criminal record information from the state Criminal Information Center. May obtain record only after a conditional offer of employment is made and applicant has given written authorization on a signed, notarized release form.

Rights of employees and applicants: Release form must advise applicant of right to appeal any of the findings in the record.

Virginia

Va. Code Ann. § 19.2-392.4

Rules for employers: May not require an applicant to disclose information about any criminal charge that has been expunged.

Rights of employees and applicants: Need not refer to any expunged charges if asked about criminal record.

Washington

Wash. Rev. Code Ann. §§ 43.43.815, 9.94A.640(3), 9.96.060(3), 9.96A.020; Wash. Admin. Code § 162-12-140

Rules for employers:

- **Arrest records.** Employer who asks about arrests must ask whether the charges are still pending, have been dismissed, or led to conviction that would adversely affect

State Laws on Employee Arrest and Conviction Records (cont'd)

job performance, and whether the arrest occurred within the last ten years.

- **Convictions.** Employer who obtains a conviction record must notify employee within 30 days of receiving it and must allow the employee to examine it. May make an employment decision based on a conviction only if it is less than 10 years old and the crime involves behavior that would adversely affect job performance.

Rights of employees and applicants: If a conviction record is cleared or vacated, may answer questions as though the conviction never occurred. A person convicted of a felony cannot be refused an occupational license unless the conviction is less than 10 years old and the felony relates specifically to the occupation or business.

Special situations: Employers are entitled to obtain complete criminal record information for positions that require bonding, or that have access to trade secrets, confidential or proprietary business information, money, or items of value.

Agency guidelines for preemployment inquiries: Washington Human Rights Commission, "Preemployment Inquiry Guide," at search.leg.wa.gov/wslwac/WAC%20162%20%20TITLE/WAC%20162%20-%2012%20%20CHAPTER/WAC%20162%20-%2012%20%20Chapter.htm.

West Virginia

Agency guidelines for preemployment inquiries: West Virginia Bureau of Employment Programs, "Pre-Employment Inquiries Technical Assistance Guide," at www.wvbep.org/bep/Bepeeo/empinqu.htm. The state's website says that employers can only make inquiries about convictions directly related to the job.

Wisconsin

Wis. Stat. §§ 111.31, 111.335

Rules for employers: It is a violation of state civil rights law to discriminate against an employee on the basis of a prior arrest or conviction record.

- **Arrest records.** May not ask about arrests unless there are pending charges.
- **Convictions.** May not ask about convictions unless charges substantially relate to job.

Special situations: Employers are entitled to obtain complete criminal record information for positions that require bonding and for burglar alarm installers.

Agency guidelines for preemployment inquiries: Wisconsin Department of Workforce Development, Equal Rights Division, Civil Rights Bureau, "Fair Hiring & Avoiding Loaded Interview Questions," dwd.wisconsin.gov/dwd/publications/erd/pdf/erd_4825_pweb.pdf.

Current as of February 2008

Driving Records

If your employee will be required to drive as part of the job duties, you would be wise to check his or her driving record. You don't want a habitual speeder, or someone with a suspended license, to do any driving for your business.

You can order a driver's record from your state's motor vehicle department, but you may need to pay a small fee to obtain it. In some states, only the driver can obtain his or her own driving record. If that's the case in your state, you'll need to ask the applicant to order the record and bring it to you.

Making a Job Offer

Once you know who you'd like to hire, there are several ways to offer the job. If you prefer to do it orally, you can do it at the end of an interview, at another face-to-face meeting, or by phone. You can also make the offer in writing—by mail, fax, or email. Or you might combine two methods by delivering a written job offer at a face-to-face meeting.

> **CAUTION**
>
> **Be careful not to make promises of job security.** However you choose to make the job offer, be careful what you promise. Avoid saying anything that might be taken as a guaranty of long-term employment, which might jeopardize the at-will employment relationship that allows to fire freely.
>
> Sometimes, the person you really want to hire for the job will push for a promise of job security. This might happen, for example, if your preferred candidate would have to leave another good job to come work for you, or move from another city to take the job. If job security becomes a part of the negotiations and you're inclined to offer it, see an experienced employment lawyer for help in writing up the arrangements.

Putting a job offer in writing helps prevent any misunderstanding about the terms and conditions of employment. Written offers should include:

- the title of the position
- the date the job begins
- the starting rate of pay
- a description of any job benefits
- a statement that you've made no oral commitments, and
- a reminder that the position is at-will.

State the amount of pay in terms of dollars per hour, week, or month. Avoid stating it as an annual amount, lest the employee treat that as a promise that the employment will last for at least one year.

Employers sometimes make a job contingent on the results they get from checking references, but the better practice is to wait until you've done all your checking and are confident you want this person as your employee.

Sample Job Offer

September 10, 20xx

Ms. Samantha Brighton
7451 Hummingbird Way
Anycity, USA 12345

Dear Ms. Brighton:

I am impressed with your credentials and enthusiasm, and am pleased to offer you a full-time position as a Graphic Designer with Manchester Enterprises LLC. I look forward to your beginning to work on September 17, 20xx.

Your starting rate of pay will be $700 per week, and you will receive health care benefits under the Green Star HMO plan. You will earn one paid vacation day for each month of work.

While I hope that your employment works out, be aware that you are an at-will employee. You have the right to end your employment at any time for any reason or for no reason; Manchester Enterprises LLC has the same right. Only I, as president of Manchester Enterprises LLC, can change this relationship, and any such change must be in writing.

Manchester Enterprises LLC has made no commitments to you—either orally or in writing—other than those contained in this letter. If this offer of employment is acceptable to you, please sign a copy and return it to me before September 17, 20xx.

On your first day of work, we will have to complete a bit of paperwork, including Form I-9, Employment Eligibility Verification, which the federal government requires. I'll need to see and photocopy the ID documents that you select from the enclosed list. Please remember to bring these documents.

I look forward to working with you.

Sincerely,

Brad Manchester

Brad Manchester
President, Manchester Enterprises LLC

Acceptance of Job Offer

I accept your offer of employment. I understand that my employment is at-will, and that either you or I can end my employment at any time, for any reason or for no reason. You have not made any oral commitments to me concerning my employment.

Signature: *Kelly Brighton*

Date: *September 12, 20xx*

Keep the copy that the employee has signed in his or her personnel file. (See Chapter 8, "Maintaining Employee Files.") Then you'll have proof that the employee received the letter and accepted its terms.

> **TIP**
>
> As described in detail in Chapter 7, "Completing Required Paperwork," your employee will be required to present documents that establish identity and eligibility to work in the United States, such as a passport or a valid driver's license and Social Security card. The list of acceptable documents is reproduced in Chapter 7. You might want to inform the employee of the need to bring the required documents on the first day of work.

Rejecting Applicants

It's good manners and just plain humane to let unsuccessful applicants know you've hired someone else for the job. But it's best to be simple and straightforward about it. Your intent is just to inform the applicant to continue looking elsewhere. You don't have to go into detail about why you made the decision not to hire.

If an applicant presses for an explanation, just say: "I hired someone who, in my judgment, is more appropriate for the job." Don't be swayed if an applicant requests more details, claiming that would help hone job-seeking skills. That may be a laudable motive, but yielding to the rejected applicant's request can be dangerous for a rejecting employer. The applicant may use your words to argue that you violated an antidiscrimination law, or acted illegally in some other way.

Here an example of a letter you might use to tell an applicant that you've hired someone else.

Sample Rejection Letter

September 15, 20xx

Peter Beck

307 Seventh Avenue

Anycity, USA 12345

Dear Mr. Beck:

Thank you for meeting with me last Thursday to discuss the opening for a Graphic Designer. You were among several fine people who applied. I wanted to let you know that I selected another applicant for the position.

It was a pleasure meeting with you, and I wish you the best in your job search.

Sincerely,

Brad Manchester

Brad Manchester

President, Manchester Enterprises LLC

It's a good idea to keep all applications and rejection letters on file for at least a year. And maintaining such paperwork files can be essential if anyone later challenges your hiring process as being unfair.

TIP

A personal letter says it best. Rejecting a job applicant by email is cold and impersonal. Doing it by phone forces the applicant to respond instantly and awkwardly to disappointing news—perhaps in the presence of other people. A letter avoids both of these problems.

Offering Noncompete and Nondisclosure Agreements

Some employers require employees to sign a noncompete agreement in which the employee promises not to work for or own a competing business during the term of employment and for a year or two beyond. Such a requirement may appeal to you if you'll be investing a great deal of time and money in training your employee, and feel that he or she might later be a competitive threat to your business. Most states will enforce a carefully worded noncompete agreement, but other states, such as California, will not—with the courts there holding that these agreements unfairly impede an employee's ability to earn a living.

Other employers also demand a nondisclosure agreement in which the employee promises not to use confidential business information for personal benefit. You might consider requiring such an agreement if your employee will have access to proprietary information that gives your business a competitive advantage—for example, unique formulas or processes, marketing plans, or lists of customers or suppliers that you have cultivated.

It's highly unlikely that you'll feel it necessary to ask for either a noncompete or nondisclosure agreement from your first employee, and these agreements should be used sparingly. But you might want to consider using either or both of them in the specialized circumstances described.

> **EXAMPLE:** Carla and Al hire Frank to help them run their self-storage business. They spend hundreds of hours training him—and thousands of dollars sending him to an out-of-state seminar. Frank learns all the aspects of the business. Then, two years later, he quits and opens his own, similar business located just a mile from theirs. Carla and Al discover that Frank has taken their customer list, their business plan, and other sensitive company information. Frank has sent letters to all of Carla and Al's customers offering them a special bargain rate if they'll switch over to his facility. If Frank had signed noncompete and nondisclosure agreements when he was hired, Carla and Al would now have a firm legal basis to go to court seeking an order closing down Frank's new venture—and perhaps they would receive monetary damages as well.

If you do decide to require either a noncompete agreement or a nondisclosure agreement, discuss this with the applicant during the job interview, or when you make a job offer. You don't want your requirement to come as a surprise.

SEE AN EXPERT

To be on the safe side, see a lawyer for help in crafting noncompete and nondisclosure agreements. ●

Preparing for Your Employee's First Day

Your employee's first day can be an exciting time for both of you. You have reached a landmark in your business career—becoming an employer for the first time, responsible for supervising another person, and meeting a payroll. Don't be surprised if you feel a bit nervous as well. But remember, too, that your employee is embarking on a new venture, and likely to feel equal measures of hope and anxiety. This chapter gives tips for easing the angst on both sides.

This chapter also offers help with the more mundane but essential task of preparing required paperwork. At a minimum, you will need to work with three forms: the I-9 from the Office of Homeland Security, W-4 from the IRS, and the New Hire Reporting Form from your state government. This chapter gives important guidance for completing them, to help you and your new hire avoid glitches.

Finally, you'll also learn about posters you may be legally required to display in your workplace. These posters inform your employee about key laws that pertain to the working relationship and explain the employee's legal rights under them.

Welcoming Your Employee

It's up to you to set the tone to get the relationship off to a good start.

Take your time on that first day to ease into the new relationship. Do all you can to make your employee feel welcome. Explain how any workplace equipment works and describe any specific procedures that must be followed. You can also ask whether your employee has suggestions for making the workspace more comfortable. Encourage your employee to personalize that workspace, if that's feasible and appropriate in your business.

Chances are, your business is part of a community of several small businesses, so make sure your employee becomes a recognized part of that community. Introduce your new employee to people in nearby businesses who are likely to see him or her come or go each day.

To show that this is an auspicious day for both of you, offer to take your employee to lunch; it doesn't have to be at a fancy restaurant. The mere act of breaking bread together, even in a modest eatery, can help you and your employee bond.

TIP

Use business cards to extend your welcome. An especially welcoming touch on the first day is to give your employee a batch of business cards with his or her name on them. You can print these cards using your computer or, for a modest charge, have them made at a print shop or office supply store.

Completing Required Paperwork

Beyond the ceremonial beginnings, you and your new employee will need to attend to a bit of official paperwork—a chore that shouldn't take more than 15 minutes or so. In particular, you will need to complete three government-related forms—each of them described below, with tips for completing and handling them.

Checklist of Paperwork for Hiring Your First Employee

The chart below lists the documents you may need, and the chapter in this book that contains detailed explanations of each of them. Note that some forms are required and others are optional.

Document	Required or Optional	Where to Find More Information
Application for Employer ID Number (Form SS-4)	Required	Chapter 5
Job Description	Optional	Chapter 5
Job Application	Optional	Chapter 5
Various Consents for Release of Information	Required (if doing a background check)	Chapter 6
Job Offer Letter	Optional	Chapter 6
Employment Eligibility Verification (Form I-9)	Required	Chapter 7
Employee's Withholding Allowance Certificate (Form W-4)	Required	Chapter 7
New Hire Reporting Form	Required	Chapter 7
Noncompete Agreement	Optional	Chapter 6
Nondisclosure Agreement	Optional	Chapter 6

Form I-9, Employment Eligibility Verification

Federal law requires employers to hire only people who may legally work in the United States: citizens and nationals, lawful permanent residents, and aliens authorized to work. To help remove employment as a magnet that attracts people to live in the United States illegally, the federal government requires all employers and employees, including employees who are U.S. citizens to complete Form I-9. Upon request, you must provide your employee's completed form to agents of the U.S. Department of Labor or the Department of Homeland Security.

Form I-9 has three sections. The instructions below will help you ensure that each section is completed correctly. Print out the form and follow along as you complete it.

RESOURCE

To download a Form I-9, go to www.uscis.gov/files/form/i-9.pdf. Be sure to print out the initial instruction page as well as the lists of Acceptable Documents that follows the one-page form. You'll need to give both pages to the employee when completing the form.

Section 1: Employee Information and Verification

The employee completes and signs this first section, which includes checking a box to indicate citizenship or work status. You, as the employer, must see that this is done when employment begins. It's also your job to see that Section 1 is filled in properly. Make sure that all the spaces contain appropriate and legible information.

An employee who can't complete Section 1 alone can get help from a preparer or translator. A preparer may be appropriate if your employee is not fully literate; a translator may be appropriate if your employee is not fluent in English. The preparer or translator must complete and sign the certification portion of Section 1, but the worker must still sign in the space for employee's signature.

You can find a preparer or translator to assist your employee. You can also let him or her make those arrangements, in which case you should let your employee know about the I-9 requirements as soon as possible because the form must be completed within three business days of the first day on the job.

If you feel qualified to do so, you can help your employee complete Section 1. If you do, you'll need to complete the Preparer/Translator Certification portion.

Section 2: Employer Review and Verification

You must complete and sign this section. Within three business days of the date employment starts, you need to examine evidence of the worker's identity and employment status.

Do this by looking at documents the government has listed as acceptable proof of the employee's identity and employment eligibility, noted below. If the worker has one of the documents on List A, that will suffice. Otherwise, you'll need to see one document from List B and one from List C.

Lists of Acceptable Documents

LIST A: Documents that establish both identity and employment eligibility

1. U.S. Passport (unexpired or expired)
2. Permanent Resident Card or Alien Registration Receipt Card (Form I-551)
3. An unexpired foreign passport with a temporary I-551 stamp
4. An unexpired Employment Authorization Document that contains a photograph (Form I-766, I-688, I-688A, I-688B)
5. An unexpired foreign passport with an unexpired Arrival-Departure Record, Form I-94, bearing the same name as the passport and containing an endorsement of the alien's nonimmigrant status, if that status authorizes the alien to work for the employer.

Lists of Acceptable Documents (cont'd)

LIST B: Documents that establish identity

1. Driver's license or ID card issued by a state or outlying possession of the United States provided it contains a photograph or information such as name, date of birth, gender, height, eye color and address

2. ID card issued by federal, state or local government agencies or entities, provided it contains a photograph or information such as name, date of birth, gender, height, eye color and address

3. School ID card with a photograph

4. Voter's registration card

5. U.S. Military card or draft record

6. Military dependent's ID card

7. U.S. Coast Guard Merchant Mariner Card

8. Native American tribal document

9. Driver's license issued by a Canadian government authority.

For people under age 18 who are not able to present a document listed above:

10. School record or report card

11. Clinic, doctor or hospital record

12. Day-care or nursery school record.

LIST C: Documents that Establish Employment Eligibility

1. U.S. Social Security card issued by the Social Security Administration (other than a card stating it is not valid for employment)

2. Certification of Birth Abroad issued by the Department of State (Form FS-545 or Form DS-1350)

3. Original or certified copy of a birth certificate issued by a state, county, municipal authority or outlying possession of the United States bearing an official seal

4. Native American tribal document

5. U.S. citizen ID card (Form I-197)

6. ID card for use of resident citizen in the United States (Form I-179)

7. Unexpired employment authorization document issued by the Department of Homeland Security (other than those listed under List A).

CAUTION

You can't specify which documents you'll accept. Your employee is free to select from among the items on the government's list. This is one good reason to print out the list of acceptable documents when you print out the Form I-9.

Make sure the employee brings you original documents, though it's all right to accept a certified copy of a birth certificate. You must honor documents that reasonably appear to be genuine and to relate to the employee. You can make photocopies for your own files if you wish; it's not required, but it's a good idea. If you do make a copy, use it only for employment verification, and keep with Form I-9.

In Section 2, note the documents you've examined. Then sign the form.

TIP

What to do if the employee needs more time. If the employee can't present the necessary documents within the three-day period, ask for a receipt showing that he or she has applied for them. The employee then will have 90 days to bring you the actual documents.

Special Rules for Employees Under Age 18

An employee who is younger than 18 years of age may not be able to present the documents specified on Lists A and B. If so, here's what to do:

- Have a parent or guardian complete Section 1 and write "Individual under age 18" in the space for the employee's signature.
- Have the parent or guardian complete the Preparer/Translator Certification block.
- Write "Individual under age 18" in Section 2, List B, in the space after the words "Document #."
- Require the minor to present a List C document showing employment eligibility; record the required information in the appropriate space in Section 2.

If your employee turns 18 while working for you, you needn't take any additional steps regarding Form I-9.

Section 3: Updating and Reverification

Don't worry about this section now. You'll only use it if you need to update or reverify the worker's status. This might happen, for example, when the expiration date for work authorization, as disclosed in Section 1, has been reached. It might also happen if you rehire the employee within three years of the date that Form I-9 was originally completed.

What to Do With the Completed Form I-9

Place the completed form—along with any photocopies of related documents—in a file that's separate from other employee records. You must keep this file for three years after the hire date, or one year after the employment ends—whichever is later.

> **CAUTION**
>
> **The importance of keeping the information separate.** The requirement that information related to Form I-9 must be kept separate from other employee records is a serious one. (See Chapter 8 for a detailed discussion of the reasoning for this—and the mechanics of keeping the records separate.)

> **RESOURCE**
>
> For more information, see Publication M-274, *Handbook for Employers: Instructions for Completing Form I-9*. It's available online at www. uscis.gov/files/nativedocuments/m-274.pdf.

Form W-4, Employee's Withholding Allowance Certificate

This form helps you determine how much federal income tax to withhold from the employee's paychecks.

> **RESOURCE**
>
> To download a copy of Form W-4 for your employee to complete, go to www.irs.gov/pub/irs-pdf/fw4.pdf.

The employee fills out lines 1 through 7, indicating the number of dependents and whether you should withhold any additional federal income tax. The employee must then sign and date the form.

> **RESOURCE**
>
> There is a withholding calculator available at www.irs.gov/ individuals/employees/index.html that can help your employee determine how many withholding allowances to claim. The calculator is a soothing resource for an employee who knows little or nothing about income tax withholding.

What to Do With the Completed Form W-4

You get the filled-in part of the form—that is, the bottom of the first page. The employee gets the rest.

Have your part of Form W-4 readily available when it's time to write paychecks. Notice that just beneath the employee portion of the form there are lines 8, 9, and 10 calling for employer information. You can leave these lines blank for now. You'll only need to complete these items if the IRS asks to see a copy of the form. This can happen if the IRS wants to make sure that your employee has directed you to withhold a sufficient amount. But in reality, the IRS rarely asks to see Form W-4.

Updating Form W-4

Your employee may need to update the Form W-4 occasionally, as personal income and the withholding preference may change from time to time.

To ensure that the information on the form remains accurate, each December, ask if your employee would like to complete a new W-4 to take effect in the coming year.

Generally, if you don't receive an updated W-4, you'll continue to use the most recent one.

There is one major exception: Your employee may have claimed an exemption from income tax withholding on line 7 of Form W-4. If so, you'll follow those instructions, though you'll still need to deduct the employee's share of Social Security and Medicare taxes. (See Chapter 10 for details on this deduction.)

However, a W-4 that claims an exemption from income tax withholding is valid for only one calendar year. It expires on February 15 of the following year. If you haven't received a new W-4 from your employee by then, you'll need to start withholding income tax.

> ⓘ **CAUTION**
>
> **Check your state law for additional requirements.** Usually the federal Form W-4 is sufficient for state withholding taxes, but some states require employees to complete a separate form in addition to the federal one. This typically occurs when a state's system for determining withholding allowances is different than the federal government's. Check with your state's revenue department.

New Hire Reporting Form

The federal government, through its Administration for Children and Families, has enlisted the help of employers in locating parents who owe child support. To that end, shortly after you hire a new employee, you must complete a New Hire Reporting Form and submit it to a designated agency in your state, which uses it to locate parents who are delinquent in paying child support. Enforcement officials can then issue or obtain an income-withholding order—the most effective means of collecting child support.

The reporting program is especially helpful when one parent lives in a different state from the child. Your state agency also passes the information to the National Directory of New Hires, which compares it with child support information from other states. When a match is found, the information is given to enforcement officials in the other state. Some states also use the new hire data to prevent improper payment of workers' compensation, unemployment benefits, or public assistance payments.

All employers, regardless of size, must complete and submit the New Hire Reporting Form—and you must complete one for every new hire, whether or not the employee claims to be a parent.

Each state has its own version of a New Hire Reporting Form. To find your state's form and requirements, go to the website operated by the U.S. Department of Health & Human Services at www.acf.hhs.gov/programs/cse/newhire/employer/contacts/nh_matrix.htm. The forms for most states are available online.

All states require the employee's name, address, Social Security number, and date of hire, as well as your business's name, address, and federal employer ID number. Some states require additional information.

Federal law requires that you submit the completed form within 20 days after the worker becomes your employee. Some states have a shorter filing deadline. (The Department of Health & Human Service's website mentioned above provides links to state-specific information.) It's a good idea to retain a copy of the completed form in the employee's file, just in case there's a question later.

Kids Are Reaping the Benefits

Congress included the new hire reporting requirements in its 1996 welfare reform legislation. A major focus of the legislation was parents' responsibility to support their children.

It is estimated that more than 30% of child support cases involve parents who don't live in the same state as their children. The national scope of the reporting requirements has enabled child support enforcement agencies to obtain child support orders, or to enforce existing orders in situations that would have been impossible in the past. The Administration for Children and Families credits the reporting system for tens of millions of dollars in new child support collections.

The program shouldn't be burdensome for you. Most of the required information is already collected when your employee completes Form W-4.

To allay concerns about the security and privacy of the new hire data, federal law requires all states to establish safeguards for the confidential information on the New Hire Reporting Form. The state agencies must use secure and dedicated lines to transmit data to the National Directory of New Hires. The government claims that access to the information is heavily restricted.

Required Posters

The federal government and most state governments require you to display certain posters in the workplace—and you should have these in place by your employee's first day on the job. These posters are intended to inform workers of their legal rights in the workplace.

> **TIP**
>
> **Display required posters where your employee can readily see them.** Putting the posters in a private office that your employee will rarely enter would not be sufficient to meet legal requirements. Putting them near the place where your employee will hang a jacket or store personal items should do the trick. Since most small businesses occupy scaled-down quarters which are fully accessible to an employee, it should be easy to display the posters where the employee will see them.

It's easy to find out what federal posters your business will need and to obtain copies of them. Go to the "Poster Advisor" operated by the U.S. Department of Labor at www.dol.gov/elaws/asp/posters/industry.asp.

It will walk you through a series of questions, starting with: "What best describes the nature of your business?" You'll mark one of many choices, such as Retail trade, Service, Professional, or Transportation.

The next screen asks how many people you employ; mark "less than 14."

Then you'll see a screen that asks, "Does your organization or business receive goods or information from businesses or organizations in other states or sell (or send) goods or information to other states?" Mark "yes," because, at the very least, your business likely receives information by mail or over the Internet from businesses in other states.

The next three screens ask you to specify:

• the state in which your business is located

• whether you have contracts or subcontracts with the federal government, and

• whether your annual gross volume of sales or business is more than $500,000.

Based on your answers to all these questions, the website will indicate what federal posters you need—and will also specify how to get them, usually by simply printing them out.

A typical one-person business will need to display three federal posters that inform your employee about rights and responsibilities under the:

- **Employee Polygraph Protection Act**, which is especially important if you require a lie detector test

- **Fair Labor Standards Act**, detailing federal minimum wage, and the overtime pay requirements, and

- **Uniformed Services Employment and Reemployment Act**, explaining rights if the employee leaves the job to perform military service.

In some states, you'll need to display a federal poster informing your employee about rights under the Occupational Safety and Health Act (OSHA). In others, you'll need to display a state OSHA poster; the federal "Poster Advisor" will provide a link to the appropriate state site.

CAUTION

Check state requirements for posters. You may need to display state employment posters in addition to a state OSHA poster. Check with your state's labor department to learn what posters are required and to find out how to get them. For contact information, go to www.dol.gov/esa/contacts/state_of.htm.

CAUTION

Beware of poster purveyors. Watch out for companies that sell poster sets—often laminated. This may sound like a convenience, but the posters are often overpriced, and often out of date. Many companies offer poster sets as a marketing device; they add you to a customer list and try to sell you a new set every year, whether or not you need it. To catch you unaware, some companies strongly imply that they're part of a governmental agency and that you'll face fines if you do not purchase the posters they're offering. Don't fall for these fraudulent solicitations or incur unnecessary costs for posters.

Other Possible Paperwork

The start-up paperwork discussed so far is required by various laws. But you may also want to consider some additional items on your employee's first day on the job—or shortly afterward—that will make it easier to run the administrative end of your business in the long run.

Contact Information

You may want to gather complete contact information from your employee if you haven't already captured this data. For example, you may want to get the employee's home address, phone numbers (land line and cell phone), email address, and the name and phone number of an emergency contact.

Enrollment Documents

There may be forms or documents the employee must complete to take part in various work-related benefits and activities.

For example, a health care plan, a retirement savings plan, or other benefits that you offer will likely have paperwork for a new hire to complete.

You may also have sign-up forms for work-related associations or for a publication you'd like the employee to receive.

An employee who will be parking in a nearby lot or garage may need to complete a form indicating the make, model, and license number of the car.

And if you'll be sending the employee to a training seminar, there may be registration forms to complete.

> **CAUTION**
>
> **Don't overwhelm your new employee with paperwork.** Not all documents and sign-ups are high priority. Save the nonessential paperwork for later rather than overwhelm your new hire with too much mundane paperwork.

Policy and Procedures Manual

You may want to write up information and describe some work-related procedures to help your employee learn the job quickly and perform more efficiently. But don't go overboard by including rigid work rules for your employee to obey. Instead, emphasize the practical aspects of the job.

For an office job, for example, you might provide instructions for answering the phone, ordering supplies, locating forms and filling them out, and finding addresses and phone numbers for key customers and suppliers. In a retail setting, you might include information on opening and closing the business, complying with credit policies, and handling returns. You can also include information about business hours and vacation and sick days.

In brief, include anything you think the employee might need handy access to that might not be obvious. You can also encourage your employee to make suggestions for changes to the policies and procedures once he or she has been on the job for a while.

Down the Road, Consider a Full-Fledged Employee Handbook

If your business grows and you hire more employees, you may find it helpful to develop a longer and more formal employee handbook.

The policies and procedures that you and your employee develop can give you a good start. Your employee handbook should cover employee benefits, workplace safety, your employees' responsibilities to the business, warnings against discrimination and harassment, protecting confidential information, and email and computer guidelines.

For in-depth guidance, see *Create Your Own Employee Handbook: A Legal and Practical Guide,* by Lisa Guerin & Amy DelPo (Nolo). It comes with a CD-ROM that enables you to quickly prepare a handbook tailored to your workplace.

Maintaining Employee Files

A long with the hope and help that a new employee can offer your business comes a new responsibility for you: collecting, organizing, and storing related paperwork—some of it required by law, some gathered merely to ease administrative headaches.

For example, as part of the hiring process, you may prepare or receive documents such as a job description, job application, or offer of employment. (See Chapters 5 and 6 for details on these.) And as part of the employee's first day on the job, you'll likely collect three federally mandated documents: Form I-9, Form W-4, and the New Hire Reporting Form. (See Chapter 7 for complete explanations of these forms and requirements.)

It's important to preserve and organize all this paperwork so you can find it when you need it. For example, good records can be a lifesaver if your employee sues you, or if the government investigates a possible violation of a statute or an administrative regulation. You may need your records to help prove that you acted legally and didn't treat your employee unfairly. You can face a nightmare if you've lost key records— or never prepared them in the first place. Also, starting out with good records for your first employee will enable you to put a system in place that will make it easy to maintain good records as your business grows and you hire more employees.

This chapter explains what documents you must keep and the best way to store and manage them. You'll also learn some precautions to take concerning your employee files. For example, you must preserve the privacy of the information and ensure that information in them is accurate and fair.

Employee Files

You'll need to maintain at least two separate files for your employee: one for most basic information and documents and one for Form I-9 documents. And if you obtain any medical information about your employer, you'll need a third separate file. Documents related to Form I-9 or the employee's medical status require a high degree of confidentiality, which means you will have to observe some special rules for how you arrange and store them.

The Main File

A letter-sized manila file folder should be sufficient to hold the main records pertaining to your employee. If you need more room, you can use an expandable pouch. Most small businesses have one or more file drawers for storing business-related documents. That would be a good place to keep the employee's file—especially if the drawer holding the file can be locked.

There are a number of documents you may have collected during the hiring process that are appropriate to retain in your employee's main file.

- **Job description.** Perhaps you used a written description of job duties and qualifications needed as the basis for a Help Wanted ad or as a checklist during the job interview. (See Chapter 5.)

- **Job application.** When your employee was still an applicant, you may have asked for a complete job application listing individual education, skills, job experience, and names of references. (See Chapter 5.)

- **Résumé.** The employee may have given you a résumé instead of—or in addition to—a job application.

- **Credit report.** If the job involves significant financial duties, you may have ordered a credit report before you hired your employee. (See Chapter 6.)

- **Offer of employment.** You may have given your employee a written employment offer. (See Chapter 6.)

- **IRS Form W-4.** You should have this federally required form, which all new hires must complete, and which gives you the information you need to compute the amount of income tax to withhold from your employee's paychecks. (See Chapters 7 and 10.)

- **Contact information.** You may have asked your employee to provide contact information—for example, a home phone number, cell phone number, email address, and name and phone number of someone to call in an emergency.

- **Sign-up forms for employee benefits.** The employee may have signed forms to enroll in benefit programs such as health care insurance or a retirement account. (See Chapter 4.)

- **New Hire Reporting Form.** This is the form that you submitted to a designated state agency to help government authorities trace people to ensure they fulfill their child support obligations. (See Chapter 7.)

- **Receipt for employee handbook.** If you prepared an employee handbook—a rarity for a business with just one employee—you probably had your employee acknowledge in writing that he or she received a copy.

- **Employment contract.** If your employee insisted on job security, you and the employee may have signed a contract. (See Chapter 6.)

- **Noncompete agreement.** You may have asked your employee to sign an agreement not to compete with your business while working for you and for a specified period afterward. (See Chapter 6.)

- **Nondisclosure agreement.** If you'll be revealing sensitive information to your employee, especially information that gives you a competitive edge, you may have had your employee agree in writing to keep the information confidential and not use it for personal benefit. (See Chapter 6.)

As time goes by, you may acquire additional documents that are worth keeping in your employee's main file:

- **Performance evaluations.** Written evaluations inform your employee about the areas in which performance is just fine—and those in which you'd like to see improvement. And if your employee is seriously underperforming, a written evaluation provides a clear and specific warning that the job is on the line. (See Chapter 13.)

- **Complaints and compliments.** Both positive and negative comments from customers, clients, suppliers, and coworkers can be useful reminders when you're considering a pay raise—or when evaluating whether your employee is doing a good job.

- **Warnings and disciplinary actions.** Similar to performance evaluations, documenting the actions you've taken in response to performance problems can help demonstrate your fairness as an employer, and help provide a record that you didn't fire the employee unfairly or for an illegal reason.

- **Wage and hour documents.** The Fair Labor Standards Act—the federal law governing wages and hours—requires you to maintain certain records on most employees. You can keep these in your employee's main file or, if you find it more convenient, in a separate payroll file. (See Chapter 10 for details on wage and hour record keeping requirements.)

> **CAUTION**
>
> **Base opinions on solid facts.** As explained in detail below, your employee may have the legal right to see the contents of the employment file. Unsubstantiated criticism in an employee file might affect your employee's morale—or, worse, spur legal action based on some perceived wrong. And bear in mind that in a lawsuit, your employee's file likely will be Exhibit A at the trial. You want to be sure that a judge or a jury would not gain the impression that you harbor hostility toward your employee—or former employee—or have acted vindictively by loading a file with questionable information.

The Separate Files

Two kinds of records should be kept in separate files—apart from one another and from an employee's main file: Form I-9, and any medical records relating to an employee with a disability.

Form I-9, Employment Eligibility Verification

As explained in Chapter 7, federal law requires you and your employee to complete this form, even if the employee is a U.S. citizen. You must keep the completed version on file for three years after the employee's hire date, or one year after the employment ends—whichever is later.

You should also keep a photocopy of the documents the employee showed you as evidence of eligibility to work in the United States.

No law requires you to keep these records in a separate file, but it's a good idea to do so. The Department of Homeland Security and the U.S. Department of Labor have the right to see your employee's Form I-9. By keeping a separate file for Form I-9, a government inspector who drops in to check the I-9 won't have easy access to other, personal information about your business and your employee.

Medical Information

It's unlikely that you'll acquire information about the physical or mental health of your first employee, but it's possible. You might receive such information, for example, if you required a preemployment medical exam, or if the employee had to reveal medical information in signing up for health care coverage.

Both the Americans With Disabilities Act (ADA) and the Family and Medical Leave Act (FMLA) include strict rules for maintaining the confidentiality of an employee's medical information. Although these federal laws don't apply to a business with only a single employee, it's still wise to adhere to their requirements. One reason is that laws in your state that are similar to the federal statutes may apply to all businesses, regardless of size. Beyond that, it's most humane to respect your employee's privacy regarding medical matters—and it's helpful to have a good system in place if your staff grows larger.

With this in mind, keep medical information separate from nonmedical records, and store the medical records in a locked cabinet. And be careful about disclosing the information to other people. It's best to allow only one person in your workplace to have access to the information. In a small business, this usually means just you or a co-owner if there is one.

The law limits those entitled to learn about medical information to:

• supervisors who must know about necessary restrictions on your employee's duties and about necessary accommodations—though this may not be relevant for a single-employee business

- first aid and safety workers who may need to administer emergency treatment, and
- government and insurance company personnel who require the information for business purposes.

Otherwise, keep medical information confidential.

 CAUTION

The law and the IRS impose some additional record keeping.
Bear in mind that the Fair Labor Standards Act requires you to keep detailed records on your employee's work hours and earnings. (See Chapter 10 for more on this.) And the IRS also requires you to keep records of payroll taxes. (See Chapter 11.) While these records are not technically part of your employee files, you may want to keep them in mind as part of the records and files you must keep organized and on hand once you hire an employee.

Protecting Your Employee's Privacy

While you need to be especially careful about safeguarding medical records, it's good practice to keep other employee records confidential as well. This can go a long way toward building goodwill and trust in the workplace, especially if you tell your employee about the steps you take to protect individual privacy.

You may decide to keep all employee records—not just medical information—under lock and key. But at the very least, store the nonmedical records in a place outsiders can't easily access. Never store medical information on a computer. And if you put some nonmedical information on your computer, make sure it is password-protected so that only you—or a co-owner with a need to know—can view the files.

Before you give out employee information to outsiders, seek your employee's written consent.

As a related issue, take steps to protect your employee's Social Security number. It is on several documents, such as Form W-4 and Form I-9.

Unscrupulous people use Social Security numbers for identity theft and other scams. So don't reveal a Social Security number to anyone without the employee's permission. Never publicly display a Social Security number, print it on an identification card, or transmit it over the Internet unless the connection is secure or password-protected. Several states have specific laws that protect the privacy of Social Security numbers.

RESOURCE

For more information about Social Security numbers and privacy, go to www.epic.org/privacy/ssn.

Employee Access to Personnel Files

Many state laws require you to let an employee see his or her personnel file.

While the extent of the employee's rights varies from state to state, most laws control:

• whether and how employees and former employees can get access

• whether employees are entitled to copies of files, and

• how employees can contest and correct information in the files.

For specifics on state rules, see the chart "State Laws on Employee Access to Personnel Records," below.

TIP

Giving access usually makes sense. Even if the law in your state doesn't require you to show your employee his or her file, you may want to do it anyway if the employee requests it. It usually seems fair and honest to do so.

State Laws on Employee Access to Personnel Records

This chart deals with only those states that authorize access to personnel files. Generally, an employee is allowed to see evaluations, performance reviews, and other documents that determine a promotion, bonus, or raise; access usually does not include letters of reference, test results, or records of a criminal or workplace violation investigation. Under other state laws, employees may have access to their medical records and records of exposure to hazardous substances; these laws are not included in this chart.

Alaska

Alaska Stat. § 23.10.430

Employers affected: All.

Employee access to records: Employee or former employee may view and copy personnel files.

Conditions for viewing records: Employee may view records during regular business hours under reasonable rules.

Copying records: Employee pays (if employer so requests).

California

Cal. Lab. Code §§ 1198.5, 432

Employers affected: All employers subject to wage and hour laws.

Employee access to records: Employee has right to inspect at reasonable intervals any personnel records relating to performance or to a grievance proceeding.

Conditions for viewing records: Employee may view records at reasonable times, during break or nonwork hours. If records are kept offsite or employer does not make them available at the workplace, then employee must be allowed to view them at the storage location without loss of pay.

Copying records: Employee has a right to a copy of any personnel document employee has signed.

Connecticut

Conn. Gen. Stat. Ann. §§ 31-128a to 31-128h

Employers affected: All.

Employee access to records: Employee has right to inspect personnel files within a reasonable time after making a request, but not more than twice a year. Employer must keep files on former employees for at least one year after termination.

Written request required: Yes.

Conditions for viewing records: Employee may view records during regular business hours in a location at or near worksite. Employer may require that files be viewed in the presence of designated official.

Copying records: Employer must provide copies within a reasonable time after receiving employee's written request; request must identify the materials employee wants copied. Employer may charge a fee that is based on the cost of supplying documents.

Employee's right to insert rebuttal: If employee disagrees with information in personnel file and cannot reach an agreement with employer to remove or correct it, employee may submit a written statement explaining her position. Rebuttal must be maintained as part of the file.

Delaware

Del. Code Ann. tit. 19, §§ 730 to 735

Employers affected: All.

State Laws on Employee Access to Personnel Records (continued)

Employee access to records: Current employee, employee who is laid off with reemployment rights, or employee on leave of absence may inspect personnel record; employee's agent is not entitled to have access to records. Unless there is reasonable cause, employer may limit access to once a year.

Written request required: At employer's discretion. Employer may require employee to file a form and indicate either the purpose of the review or what parts of the record employee wants to inspect.

Conditions for viewing records: Records may be viewed during employer's regular business hours. Employer may require that employees view files on their own time and may also require that files be viewed on the premises and in the presence of designated official.

Copying records: Employer is not required to permit employee to copy records. Employee may take notes.

Employee's right to insert rebuttal: If employee disagrees with information in personnel file and cannot reach an agreement with employer to remove or correct it, employee may submit a written statement explaining her position. Rebuttal must be maintained as part of the personnel file.

Illinois

820 Ill. Comp. Stat. §§ 40/1 to 40/12

Employers affected: Employers with five or more employees

Employee access to records: Current employee, or former employee terminated within the past year, is permitted to inspect records twice a year at reasonable intervals, unless a collective bargaining agreement provides otherwise. An employee involved in a current grievance may designate a representative of the union or collective bargaining unit, or other agent, to inspect personnel records that may be relevant to resolving the grievance. Employer must make records available within seven working days after employee makes request (if employer cannot meet deadline, an additional 7 days may be allowed).

Written request required: At employer's discretion. Employer may require use of a form.

Conditions for viewing records: Records may be viewed during normal business hours at or near worksite or, at employer's discretion, during nonworking hours at a different location if more convenient for employee.

Copying records: After reviewing records, employee may get a copy. Employer may charge only actual cost of duplication. If employee is unable to view files at worksite, employer, upon receipt of a written request, must mail employee a copy.

Employee's right to insert rebuttal: If employee disagrees with any information in the personnel file and cannot reach an agreement with employer to remove or correct it, employee may submit a written statement explaining his position. Rebuttal must remain on file with no additional comment by employer.

Iowa

Iowa Code §§ 91A.2, 91B.1

Employers affected: All employers with salaried employees or commissioned salespeople.

State Laws on Employee Access to Personnel Records (continued)

Employee access to records: Employee may have access to personnel file at time agreed upon by employer and employee.

Conditions for viewing records: Employer's representative may be present.

Copying records: Employer may charge copying fee per page that is equivalent to a commercial copying service fee.

Maine

Me. Rev. Stat. Ann. tit. 26, § 631

Employers affected: All.

Employee access to records: Within 10 days of submitting request, employee, former employee, or authorized representative may view and copy personnel files.

Written request required: Yes.

Conditions for viewing records: Employee may view records during normal business hours at the location where the files are kept, unless employer, at own discretion, arranges a time and place more convenient for employee. If files are in electronic or any other nonprint format, employer must provide equipment for viewing and copying.

Copying records: Employee is entitled to one free copy of personnel file during each calendar year, including any material added to file during that year. Employee must pay for any additional copies.

Massachusetts

Mass. Gen. Laws ch. 149, § 52C

Employers affected: All (employers with 20 or more employees must maintain personnel records for three years after termination).

Employee access to records: Employee or former employee must have opportunity to review personnel files within five business days of submitting request. (Law does not apply to tenured or tenure-track employees in private colleges and universities.)

Written request required: Yes.

Conditions for viewing records: Employee may view records at workplace during normal business hours.

Copying records: Employee must be given a copy of record within five business days of submitting a written request.

Employee's right to insert rebuttal: If employee disagrees with any information in personnel record and cannot reach an agreement with employer to remove or correct it, employee may submit a written statement explaining her position. Rebuttal becomes a part of the personnel file.

Michigan

Mich. Comp. Laws §§ 423.501 to 423.505

Employers affected: Employers with four or more employees.

Employee access to records: Current or former employee is entitled to review personnel records at reasonable intervals, generally not more than twice a year, unless a collective bargaining agreement provides otherwise.

Written request required: Yes. Request must describe the records employee wants to review.

Conditions for viewing records: Employee may view records during normal office hours either at or reasonably near the worksite. If these hours would require employee to take time off work, employer must provide another reasonable time for review.

State Laws on Employee Access to Personnel Records (continued)

Copying records: After reviewing files, employee may get a copy; employer may charge only actual cost of duplication. If employee is unable to view files at the worksite, employer, upon receipt of a written request, must mail employee a copy.

Employee's right to insert rebuttal: If employee disagrees with any information in personnel record and cannot reach an agreement with employer to remove or correct it, employee may submit a written statement explaining his position. Statement may be no longer than five 8½" by 11" pages.

Minnesota

Minn. Stat. Ann. §§ 181.960 to 181.966

Employers affected: 20 or more employees.

Employee access to records: Current employee may review files once per six-month period; former employee may have access to records once only during the first year after termination. Employer must comply with written request within seven working days (14 working days if personnel records are kept out of state). Employer may not retaliate against an employee who asserts rights under these laws.

Written request required: Yes.

Conditions for viewing records: Current employee may view records during employer's normal business hours at work site or a nearby location; does not have to take place during employee's working hours. Employer or employer's representative may be present.

Copying records: Employer must provide copies free of charge. Current employee must first review record and then submit written request for copies. Former employee must submit written request; providing former employee with a copy fulfills employer's

obligation to allow access to records.

Employee's right to insert rebuttal: If employee disputes specific information in the personnel record, and cannot reach an agreement with employer to remove or revise it, employee may submit a written statement identifying the disputed information and explaining her position. Statement may be no longer than five pages and must be kept with personnel record as long as record is maintained.

Nevada

Nev. Rev. Stat. Ann. § 613.075

Employers affected: All.

Employee access to records: An employee who has worked at least 60 days, and a former employee within 60 days of termination, must be given a reasonable opportunity to inspect personnel records.

Conditions for viewing records: Employee may view records during employer's normal business hours.

Copying records: Employer may charge only actual cost of providing access and copies.

Employee's right to insert rebuttal: Employee may submit a reasonable written explanation in direct response to any entry in personnel record. Statement must be of reasonable length; employer may specify the format; employer must maintain statement in personnel records.

New Hampshire

N.H. Rev. Stat. Ann. § 275:56

Employers affected: All.

Employee access to records: Employer must provide employees a reasonable opportunity to inspect records.

State Laws on Employee Access to Personnel Records (continued)

Copying records: Employer may charge a fee reasonably related to the cost of supplying copies.

Employee's right to insert rebuttal: If employee disagrees with any of the information in personnel record and cannot reach an agreement with the employer to remove or correct it, employee may submit a written statement of her version of the information along with evidence to support her position. Statement must be maintained as part of personnel file.

Oregon

Or. Rev. Stat. § 652.750

Employers affected: All.

Employee access to records: Within 45 days after receipt of request, employer must provide employee a reasonable opportunity to inspect personnel records used to determine qualifications for employment, promotion, additional compensation, termination, or other disciplinary action. Employer must keep records for 60 days after termination of employee.

Conditions for viewing records: Employee may view records at work site or place of work assignment.

Copying records: Within 45 days after receipt of request, employer must provide a certified copy of requested record to current or former employee (if request is made within 60 days of termination). May charge amount reasonably calculated to recover actual cost of providing copy.

Pennsylvania

43 Pa. Cons. Stat. Ann. §§ 1321 to 1324

Employers affected: All.

Employee access to records: Employer must allow employee to inspect personnel record at reasonable times. (Employee's agent, or employee who is laid off with reemployment rights or is on leave of absence, must also be given access.) Unless there is reasonable cause, employer may limit review to once a year by employee and once a year by employee's agent.

Written request required: At employer's discretion. Employer may require the use of a form as well as a written indication of the parts of the record employee wants to inspect, and the purpose of the inspection. For employee's agent: Employee must provide signed authorization designating agent; authorization must be for a specific date and must indicate the reason for the inspection or the parts of the record the agent is authorized to inspect.

Conditions for viewing records: Employee may view records during regular business hours at the office where records are maintained, when there is enough time for employee to complete the review. Employer may require that the employee or agent view records on their own time and may also require that inspection take place on the premises and in the presence of employer's designated official.

Copying records: Employer is not obligated to permit copying. Employee may take notes.

Employee's right to insert rebuttal: The Bureau of Labor Standards, after a petition and hearing, may allow employee to place a counterstatement in the personnel file, if employee claims that the file contains an error.

State Laws on Employee Access to Personnel Records (continued)

Rhode Island

R.I. Gen. Laws § 28-6.4-1

Employers affected: All.

Employee access to records: Employer must permit employee to inspect personnel files when given at least seven days' advance notice (excluding weekends and holidays). Employer may limit access to no more than three times a year.

Written request required: Yes.

Conditions for viewing records: Employee may view records at any reasonable time other than employee's work hours. Inspection must take place in presence of employer or employer's representative.

Copying records: Employee may not make copies or remove files from place of inspection. Employer may charge a fee reasonably related to cost of supplying copies.

Washington

Wash. Rev. Code Ann. §§ 49.12.240 to 49.12.260

Employers affected: All.

Employee access to records: Employee may have access to personnel records at least once a year within a reasonable time after making a request.

Employee's right to insert rebuttal: Employee may petition annually that employer review all information in employee's personnel file. If there is any irrelevant or incorrect information in the file, employer must remove it. If employee does not agree with employer's review, employee may have a statement of rebuttal or correction placed in the file. Former employee has right of rebuttal for two years after termination.

Wisconsin

Wis. Stat. § 103.13

Employers affected: All employers who maintain personnel records.

Employee access to records: Employee and former employee must be allowed to inspect personnel records within seven working days of making request. Access is permitted twice per calendar year unless a collective bargaining agreement provides otherwise. Employee involved in a current grievance may designate a representative of the union or collective bargaining unit, or other agent, to inspect records that may be relevant to resolving the grievance.

Written request required: At employer's discretion.

Conditions for viewing records: Employee may view records during normal working hours at a location reasonably near work site. If this would require employee to take time off work, employer may provide another reasonable time for review.

Copying records: Employee's right of inspection includes the right to make or receive copies. If employer provides copies, only actual cost of reproduction may be charged.

Employee's right to insert rebuttal: If employee disagrees with any information in the personnel record and cannot come to an agreement with the employer to remove or correct it, employee may submit a written statement explaining his position. Employer must attach the statement to the disputed portion of the personnel record.

Current as of February 2008

Dealing With Safety and Health Concerns

As an employer, you must provide safe and healthy working conditions as mandated by state and federal laws. For most small businesses—especially those with one or just a few employees—this usually amounts to using common sense and displaying a government poster summarizing an employee's rights. But if your business uses hazardous materials or dangerous equipment, you'll need to learn about and comply with additional specific safety and health requirements. This chapter explains the basic legal requirements and refers you to additional resources for more thorough guidance if you need it.

If, despite your best efforts, your employee gets hurt on the job or suffers a work-related illness, you'd like to feel confident that he or she won't face a financial disaster—and that you and your business won't have to pay damages that a court may award. To protect against this, you'll need to buy workers' compensation insurance, even if your state law makes this coverage optional. This chapter describes the inner workings of workers' compensation—a system designed to pay workers who become ill or injured on the job.

Finally, this chapter alerts you to laws and ordinances which, in some states or localities, require you to provide a workplace free of tobacco smoke—another health and safety matter.

The Occupational Safety and Health Act

The main federal law regulating workplace health and safety is the Occupational Safety and Health Act, or OSHA. It requires you to provide a workplace free from hazards that are likely to cause death or serious physical harm to your employee. It also requires you to meet specific safety and health standards—most of which deal with hazardous chemicals and dangerous equipment. Many states have similar laws. (See "State Safety and Health Laws," below.)

In theory, you can be heavily penalized for not complying with these safety and health requirements. But the reality is that you'll only get in trouble if your workplace conditions are highly dangerous and you've ignored complaints of warnings about them.

Health and Safety Standards

The broad mandates of OSHA are supplemented by more specific standards set by the Occupational Safety and Health Administration— also called OSHA—which is a unit of the U.S. Department of Labor.

The specific standards cover a wide range of workplace concerns, including:

- exposure to chemical hazards
- first aid and medical treatment
- noise levels
- protective gears—such as goggles, respirators, gloves, work shoes, and ear protection
- fire protection
- worker training, and
- workplace temperatures and ventilation.

Once you've had an OSHA consultation or have read up on the subject, you may be able to take a number of inexpensive measures to reduce risks to your employee.

EXAMPLE: Lars, who owns a shop that repairs and refinishes furniture, is planning to hire Edie as an assistant. In addition to using noisy power tools, Edie will be using volatile solvents to remove existing finishes before applying new ones. After evaluating the hazards to which Edie will be exposed, Lars purchases goggles, ear protectors, gloves, and a breathing mask for her. He also installs a more powerful exhaust fan to carry away particles and fumes, and he buys a comprehensive first aid kit and an industrial grade fire extinguisher.

To inform Edie about the solvents and varnishes she'll be using, he puts together a loose-leaf binder containing safety information supplied by each product's manufacturer. Finally, when Edie begins work, Lars carefully trains her in the safe use of power equipment and each of the chemicals in the shop.

Getting More Guidance on OSHA Requirements

If you're not sure whether there are conditions in your workplace that require attention, you can call an OSHA-sponsored agency in your state for a free and confidential onsite consultation. For contact information, go to www.osha.gov/dcsp/smallbusiness/consult_directory.html.

But you'll likely find all the information you need to know in one or more of the OSHA publications available at www.osha.gov.

Here are three you may find especially helpful:

- **OSHA Publication 2209,** *Handbook for Small Business.* This handbook gives you an excellent overview of the obligations for protecting your employee's safety and health, and describes the many OSHA resources you can turn to for help. Best of all, it includes extensive checklists you can use to inspect your workplace for hazards.

- **OSHA Publication 3151,** *Assessing the Need for Personal Protective Equipment.* This publication covers a wide range of clothing and equipment that can save your employee from harm, ranging from eye and hearing protection to protective gloves, hats, and shoes.

- **OSHA Publication 3084,** *Chemical Hazard Communication.* Here you can learn more about hazardous chemicals in the workplace and how to obtain and use Material Data Safety Sheets.

All of these publications are available through the OSHA website at www.osha.gov.

Hazardous Chemicals

An important OSHA goal is to protect workers from chemicals in the workplace that can harm them. The OSHA rules define "chemicals" much more broadly than common materials such as paints, fuels, and solvents that are typically stored in containers. The term includes chemicals in all physical forms: liquids, solids, gases, vapors, fumes, and mists.

To help protect workers from hazardous chemicals, the OSHA rules include a Hazard Communication Standard—a type of right-to-know obligation. Basically, it requires you to label hazardous chemicals in your workplace. About half of the states have similar requirements in addition to the federal standards. In case of a conflict, you must follow the stricter standards.

As a starting point, contact the manufacturer of any hazardous chemicals you have in your workplace. The manufacturer can supply you with Material Safety Data Sheets that describe:

• the physical hazards of the chemical, such as flammability and explosiveness

• health hazards

• how the chemical enters the body and the limits of safe exposure

• whether the chemical is known to cause cancer

• how to safely handle the chemical

• recommended protection methods, and

• first aid and emergency procedures.

Keep the safety sheets near the chemicals your employee will be using on the job. Also, keep a list of the hazardous chemicals used in your business, and label all containers. Be sure to train your employee how to use the chemicals safely.

If you're unsure about what hazardous chemicals exist in your workplace, or how best to reduce the danger to your employee, consider getting a free, confidential consultation. (See "Getting More Guidance on OSHA Requirements," above.) And if you need help in training your employee, ask the consultant about OSHA's training programs. In many cases, the OSHA consultant can provide the safety training while at your workplace.

Hazards Can Lurk Even in Office Settings

Industrial and construction jobs are not the only type of work that can endanger an employee's safety and health. As noted below, even office jobs can put an employee at risk.

Unsafe space heaters. Portable space heaters can cause a fire if not used properly. Make sure any space heater is approved for commercial use. Never place one near combustible materials, or connect it to an extension cord.

Carbonless copy paper. Certain types of carbonless copy paper can irritate skin, eyes, and the upper respiratory tract. Make sure there is adequate ventilation in your workplace, and that your employee can periodically wash away the irritants.

Loose carpeting. This can cause your employee to trip and fall. Inspect your workplace to make sure your rugs and carpets are secure.

Emissions from office equipment. Some people find that ozone emitted by a copier makes it difficult to breathe, or causes headaches and dizziness. To avoid problems, put your copier in a separate area, and make sure there is good air flow. Doing so can also help protect you and your employee from harmful toner particles that your copier may emit. And recent studies suggest that printers and fax machines also may emit dangerous particles, so it can be helpful to place this equipment in a well-ventilated area as well.

Computer hazards. An employee doing repetitive work using a computer keyboard and mouse can develop tendon and nerve problems, or even carpal tunnel syndrome. Provide an adjustable chair and encourage your employee to take regular breaks. Computer monitors can cause eye strain. See that your employee's monitor is properly positioned, and that glare is kept to a minimum.

Damaged power cords. Damaged and ungrounded power cords pose a threat of electric shock and are a fire hazard. Inspect cords for wear and tear. Don't use a plug if the third prong, used to ground the plug, has been damaged or removed.

Improper storage of heavy items. Stacks of materials or heavy items can fall on your employee. Store heavy items close to the floor, and don't exceed the safe load capacity of shelves or storage units.

Misused extension cords. Extension cords are not a good substitute for electric outlets, as they can cause a fire. Use an extension cord only temporarily, and connect it to only one device at a time.

State Safety and Health Laws

OSHA has encouraged the states to develop and operate their own health and safety programs with standards that are at least as vigorous as the federal controls.

So far, the following states are certified to enforce OSHA standards in the private sector: Alaska, Arizona, California, Hawaii, Indiana, Iowa, Kentucky, Maryland, Michigan, Minnesota, Nevada, New Mexico, North Carolina, Oregon, South Carolina, Tennessee, Utah, Vermont, Virginia, Washington, and Wyoming. You can find a current list of certified states, along with contact information for their plans, at www.osha.gov/dcsp/osp/index.html.

If your business is located in a state that has an OSHA law—even one that is not certified by the federal agency—contact your state agency to learn the standards that apply to your business.

Many state rules are stricter than the federal rules. In Minnesota, for example, the employee right-to-know law covers more that just hazardous substances; it also covers noise, heat, radiation, and infectious agents. Michigan requires employers to notify employees when a new chemical hazard is introduced in the workplace. And several states have adopted standards prohibiting the use of short-handled hoes, which can cause back problems among agricultural workers.

CAUTION

You may be required to display OSHA posters. Your business will need to display either a federal or a state poster informing employees about their OSHA rights. To learn which one you need, go to OSHA's Poster Advisor at www.dologov/elaws/asp/posters and walk through the questions you're asked. (See Chapter 7, "Required Posters," for specific tips on how to do this.) If you need a federal OSHA poster, you can print one out directly from the site. For a state OSHA poster, contact your state's labor department. You can find local contact information by going to www.osha.gov and clicking on "Services By Location."

Workers' Compensation Insurance

Every state has a workers' compensation system to ensure that employees who suffer work-related injuries or illnesses receive some replacement income and have their medical expenses paid. And in most cases, the workers' compensation system protects a participating employer from being sued for such injuries and illnesses; the worker receives payment from an insurance company or state fund, and has no further legal claims against the employer. The main exception to this protective shield is that you can still be legally liable if you *intentionally* cause an injury or illness—a highly unlikely prospect. (See "You're Still Liable for Intentional Injuries," below.)

To provide money for these benefits, almost all states require employers to buy workers' compensation insurance. Some states make the insurance optional for all employers, while a few others make it optional for businesses with one or just a few employees. It's also possible in some states for an employer to self-insure rather buy insurance, but that's not usually economically feasible for most small businesspeople.

Whatever the options are in your state, your best bet is to bite the bullet and buy the insurance to protect against the potentially devastating financial consequences of a lawsuit.

RESOURCE

To get more specific information about the workers' compensation law in your state, go to www.workerscompensation.com.

Buying Workers' Compensation Insurance

In most states, workers' compensation insurance is available only through private insurance companies. In four states—North Dakota, Ohio, Washington, and Wyoming—the insurance is available only through a state-run fund. And in the following states, you can choose between a private company and a state-run fund: Arizona, California, Colorado, Idaho, Kentucky, Maryland, Minnesota, Montana, New York, Oklahoma, Oregon, Pennsylvania, Texas, and Utah.

When you have a choice about where to obtain workers' compensation coverage—among private insurers, or between private insurers and a state fund—you can usually compare prices by placing a few phone calls. But don't be surprised if there's little or no variation in pricing. If your state allows purchasing the insurance through a private company, check with the insurance agent or broker who handles your business's property and liability insurance. It may be convenient—and cost effective—to buy all of your insurance in one place.

Benefits for Disabilities That Are Not Work-Related

Five states—California, Hawaii, New Jersey, New York, and Rhode Island—have temporary disability insurance (TDI) programs that partially replace the wages of employees who suffer injuries or illnesses that are not work-related, but prevent them from doing some or all of their normal work.

Employees may be required to contribute to the cost of this benefit, and in Hawaii, New Jersey, and Rhode Island, employers must contribute as well. The TDI mechanics vary.

To learn the requirements for your state, check the following sites:
- **California:** www.edd.ca.gov/direp/diind.htm
- **Hawaii:** www.hawaii.gov/labor/dcd/abouttdi.shtml
- **New Jersey:** http://lwd.dol.state.nj.us/labor/tdi/tdiindex.html
- **New York:** www.wcb.state.ny.us/content/main/disabilitybenefits/employer/introtolawinclude.jsp, and
- **Rhode Island:** www.dlt.ri.gov/tdi.

When looking into the TDI law in your state, be especially mindful of the types of employees who may be excluded from these programs.

The No-Fault Feature

Workers' compensation is a no-fault system, which means that if you carry the coverage, the insurance company or state fund will pay your employee certain benefits whether or not you provided a safe workplace—and whether or not your employee's own carelessness contributed to the injury or illness.

These payments will at least partially replace lost wages and also cover medical bills. Your employee won't be compensated for noneconomic damages, such as pain and suffering, or mental anguish—which might be allowed if the employee were to sue you for personal injury.

EXAMPLE: Your employee, Emily, slips on a wet spot on the workplace floor, falls down, and breaks her hip. To collect workers' compensation benefits, Emily doesn't have to prove that you were negligent in leaving water on the floor, nor must she prove that she was free of fault. Emily is automatically entitled to receive workers' compensation benefits—though she'll only collect partial compensation for her lost wages, as established by state law. And she'll collect nothing for her pain and suffering. Assuming you have purchased workers' compensation insurance, Emily won't be able to sue you or your business for the mishap.

You're Still Liable for Intentional Injuries

In most cases, accepting workers' compensation is your employee's only option when a work-related injury or illness occurs. There's a major exception, however, if you as the employer cause an injury or illness intentionally. In such situations, the employee can sue you and claim a full range of damages, including damages for pain and suffering, as well as all monetary losses.

Obviously, if you physically assault your employee, that would be an intentional action that would open the door to damages outside the workers' compensation system. But less obviously, other activities can also amount to intentional action in the eyes of the law.

For example, suppose you instruct your employee to use a piece of power equipment after you've learned that its safety features are not working, and that anyone using the equipment is likely to get hurt.

If an employee who is injured while using the equipment can provide proof of your prior knowledge, a court is likely to find that the injury was caused by your intentional actions.

⚠ **CAUTION**

Don't penalize your employee for filing a claim. In most states, it's a violation of the workers' compensation statute or public policy to retaliate against an employee for filing a workers' compensation claim. In those states, it would be illegal, for example, to fire a worker or reduce job benefits because of filing such a claim.

Tobacco Smoke in the Workplace

Most states have laws requiring employers to provide a workplace free of tobacco smoke—or imposing restrictions on tobacco smoke. For a list of those states, go to http://ash.org/smokingbans.html, a Web page maintained by a nonprofit organization, Action on Smoking and Health. In addition, many counties and cities have adopted ordinances with similar requirements. You'll find a current list at http://no-smoke .org/pdf/100ordlisttabs.pdf, a site maintained by the Americans for Nonsmokers' Rights.

Laws and ordinances regulating smoking are intended to protect the health of employees, as well as customers, clients, and business owners. Even if your business isn't legally required to ban or restrict smoking on its premises, you're free to adopt such a policy. And you're free to prohibit your employee from smoking anywhere while on the job— something to consider, for example, if your employee will be calling on customers or clients at their homes or businesses.

But don't prohibit your employee from smoking off the job as well. Such a broad prohibition can invade your employee's privacy, and is specifically barred by some state laws.

> **TIP**
>
> **Accommodating committed smokers.** You can designate a smoking room to accommodate smokers, but that can be expensive and it may be hard to confine the smoke to that room. Cruel as it may seem on a broiling summer or freezing winter day, your only solution may be to require the smokers to indulge in their habit outdoors—and away from the entrance so that smoke doesn't drift inside or offend customers or clients coming to your business place. ●

Paying Your Employee

On the surface, paying an employee may seem like a simple, straightforward task: Your employee does the work and you write a paycheck. Actually, it's a bit more complicated than that—but well within your ability to master. The possible complications come, as you may have guessed, from government regulations and requirements.

First, there are the wage and hour laws, which may regulate how much and when workers must be paid. (See Chapter 3 for details.) Then there are federal and state laws requiring an employer to deduct income and other taxes from an employee's paychecks.

In this chapter, you'll learn how to compute your employee's earnings and deduct taxes from them. (Chapter 11 covers how to remit payroll taxes to the government and how to handle the associated paperwork.) You'll also learn the right way to reimburse your employee for business expenses. Finally, this chapter discusses some record keeping duties associated with your employee's wages and hours—another requirement imposed by law.

Preparing Paychecks

There are three steps involved in preparing paychecks:

- determining how much your employee earned
- computing the deductions, and
- writing a check for the net amount.

SEE AN EXPERT

Preparing paychecks and dealing with the associated tax forms is not difficult, but you may have reasons for getting help with some or all of the work. For example, you may despise paperwork, prefer not to work with numbers, or simply lack the time or patience to handle paychecks or taxes. One solution may be to use payroll software that can crunch the numbers for you. Another is to use a payroll service such as Paychex or Intuit Payroll

Services. Or you can follow a more traditional route and hand off the work to a bookkeeper or accountant.

Step 1: Determine Earnings

It's up to you and your employee to decide how frequently he or she will be paid: weekly, biweekly, semi-monthly, or monthly. Then, when it's payroll time, you can compute how much your employee earned during the payroll period.

It's relatively simple if your employee earns a regular salary and there are no overtime or other issues that may cause the payments to vary. For example, if your employee earns $500 a week, you won't have to make earnings calculations for each paycheck. But with an employee who earns an hourly rate, works varying hours, and is entitled to overtime pay, you'll need to do a modest amount of figuring.

> EXAMPLE: An employee earns $16 an hour and is paid weekly. In the most recent payroll period, the employee worked 44 hours. The employer makes a few simple calculations to determine the week's earnings:
>
> Regular hours: 40 x $16 = $640
>
> Overtime hours: 4 x $24 =   96
>
> Total earnings: $736

Step 2: Compute Deductions

You must withhold federal income tax and Social Security and Medicare taxes from your employee's paychecks. You may also need to make deductions for any contributions to benefit programs that your employee has indicated. For example, your employee may have requested payroll deductions for a retirement plan, or for an individual share of health care insurance.

Federal Income Tax

To compute the amount of income tax you must withhold, you'll need your employee's Form W-4 (see Chapter 7), and the current year's edition of IRS Publication 15, *Circular E, Employer's Tax Guide.* Once your business has obtained an Employer Identification Number (explained in Chapter 5), the IRS should automatically send you a copy of the current *Circular E*. If you haven't received this publication, go to www.irs.gov, where you can view or download it.

At the back of the circular, you'll find tables telling you how much federal income tax to withhold. To use the tables, look at item 3 of your employee's Form W-4—specifically, at the spot where he or she should have checked one of three boxes: "Single," "Married," or "Married but withhold at the higher Single rate." Also, note the total number of dependents your employee has designated. Then find the appropriate table.

> **EXAMPLE:** An employee who earned $736 during the current week has checked "Married" on Form W-4 and has indicated three dependents. The employer goes to the table labeled "Married Persons—Weekly Payroll Period." The first column lists wages in $10 increments. The employer goes to the line for wages of at least $730 but less than $740. Reading across the page to the column giving withholding amounts for an employee with three dependents, the employer sees that $42 must be withheld from the employee's paycheck. (This is based on the 2008 circular; the amounts change annually.)

TIP

Your employee's directions, not the withholding tables, are the final word. Check item 6 of Form W-4 to see whether your employee has asked you to withhold an additional amount of income tax beyond what the tables require. This might be the case if your employee wants to cover a year-end tax bill that will include outside income—such as income from investments—or if the idea is to get a hefty tax refund.

Also, check line 7 to see whether your employee claimed an exemption from income tax withholding. In that case, don't withhold income tax—but do withhold Social Security and Medicare taxes. A W-4 indicating an income tax withholding exemption is valid for only one calendar year, and expires on February 15 of the following year. If your employee doesn't give you a new W-4 by then, withhold income tax at the single rate with no withholding allowances.

RESOURCE

If you provide benefits such as health insurance, adoption assistance, dependent care assistance, educational assistance, life insurance, meals, or commuting expenses, figuring out employment taxes can be challenging. Some benefits are treated as compensation, while others are not. *Circular E* offers only general guidance on this topic. IRS Publication 15B, *Employer Tax Guide to Fringe Benefits*, goes into much greater depth. You'll find it at www.irs.gov.

You may, however, prefer to see a tax professional to determine how the employment tax rules apply to the particular fringe benefits that you are providing.

State Income Tax

Most states have an income tax. The ones that don't are Alaska, Florida, Nevada, South Dakota, Texas, Washington, and Wyoming. Unless your business is located in one of these states, you must deduct the state tax from your employee's paycheck in addition to the amount required by the federal government.

Your state tax department can provide information and forms. For contact information, go to www.taxsites.com/agencies.html.

A few cities also impose an income tax. Your city treasurer can provide particulars.

Social Security and Medicare Taxes (FICA)

You need to withhold the employee's share of Social Security and Medicare taxes.

The employee's share and cap on earnings for those taxes changes yearly, but for 2008 the figures are:

- Social Security—6.2% of gross earnings, up to $102,000
- Medicare—1.45% of gross earnings, no cap

EXAMPLE: An employee has earned $736 during the current pay period. Here is how the employer would compute these taxes:

Social Security	6.2% x	$736	=	$45.63
Medicare	1.45% x	$736	=	10.67
Total				$62.30

Other Payroll Deductions

Your employee may have authorized other deductions such as for health care insurance or for a contribution to a retirement account.

Also, some states require deductions for items other than state income tax. For example, in California, Hawaii, New Jersey, New York, and Rhode Island, an employer must deduct money to be paid into a disability insurance fund. And in Alaska, New Jersey, Pennsylvania, and Rhode Island, an employer must deduct employee contributions to an unemployment fund.

To check on specifics for your state, go to www.sba.gov/localresources/index.html and click on the map. You'll be linked to the Small Business Administration's site for your state, where you can then pursue links to tax information.

Tips Are Subject to Withholding

You may have a business in which customers routinely tip your employee. If so—and if your employee receives $20 or more in tips during a given month—you must withhold and remit income tax and Social Security and Medicare taxes on those tips.

Your employee must report the tips to you on IRS Form 4070, *Employee's Report of Tips to Employer,* or on a similar statement, for any month in which the tips total $20 or more. Your employee must do this by the 10th of the following month. For example, an employee who receives $35 in tips in June must report those tips to you by July 10th.

Tips to be reported include both the cash given directly by customers and the tips from credit card customers that you paid over to your employee.

For more details, see *Circular E.* You'll find Form 4070 and Form 4070-A—voluntary forms on which an employee can record and report tips—in IRS Publication 1244, *Employee's Daily Record of Tips and Report to Employer.* Unlike many other IRS forms, these can actually make life easier for you and your employee.

Step 3: Write a Check

Once you know all the deductions that are required, you can prepare your employee's paycheck.

EXAMPLE: An employee has earned $736 during the current week, checked "Married" on Form W-4, and designated three dependents. The employee is also contributing $10 a week toward health insurance coverage.

The deductions might look like this:

Federal income tax	$42.00
State income tax	5.00
Social Security tax	45.63
Medicare tax	10.67
Health insurance	10.00
Total	$113.30

The employee will receive a net paycheck of $622.70 ($736.00 – $113.30).

Even though it may not be legally required that you itemize deductions, it's a good idea to do so on a paycheck stub or a separate sheet so your employee knows what you've done. Keep a record for yourself. Most payroll software will also produce these deduction records.

CAUTION

Write paychecks from your business's bank account. Your business should maintain a bank account that's separate from your personal bank account. Deposit business income into the business account—and pay business expenses, including paychecks, from it. If you commingle business and personal funds, you're likely to face accounting, tax, and legal headaches.

Reimbursing Expenses

To complete the payment picture, bear in mind that you may need to reimburse your employee for expenses you've authorized relating to your business—or you may decide to advance money to your employee for business-related expenses. For example, you may ask your employee to purchase some office supplies or a roll of stamps, or to attend a training seminar.

Basically, your business should reimburse or advance money only if your employee:

- pays or incurs deductible business expenses for your business while working as your employee

- adequately accounts to you for the expenses within a reasonable time, and

- returns any excess payments to you within a reasonable time.

To avoid any possible misunderstandings with your employee, it makes sense to put these guidelines in writing, though there is no legal requirement that you do so.

If you observe these payment guidelines, whether written or not, you will meet the IRS requirements for an "accountable plan" for reimbursements and advances. This will allow your business and your employee to reap several tax benefits, including that:

- no payroll taxes will be owed on the payments

- your employee won't have to report the payments as taxable income, and

- your business can deduct the payments as business expenses.

You can compensate your employee for business expenses by writing a check, allowing him or her to charge the expenses to your business's credit card, or by having the charges billed directly to your business. To avoid bookkeeping and tax problems, *don't* include a reimbursement or an advance in a paycheck. Write a separate check, instead. And be sure to get receipts for the expenses the employee incurs.

EXAMPLE: North Country Appraisers, LLC sends its employee Rajiv to an appraisal seminar in another city. Rajiv pays his expenses himself. Back home, Rajiv documents his expenses, noting that he spent $1,000 for airfare and a hotel room, and $500 for meals and entertainment. North Country writes a reimbursement check to Rajiv for $1,500.

In computing its taxes, North Country can deduct the $1,000 for airfare and lodging as a business expense. It can also deduct 50% of the $500 cost of meals and entertainment. Rajiv needn't treat any part of the $1,500 as income, and North Country doesn't have to include it on Rajiv's year-end W-2 or withhold any income tax, or Social Security or Medicare tax.

Your employee should give you documents confirming expenses for travel, lodging, meals, and entertainment. Another way to handle expenses is to allow your employee a fixed amount for each day's expenses—also called a per diem.

RESOURCE

For details, see IRS Publication 1542, *Per Diem Rates.* For general information on accountable plans for reimbursing employees, see Publication 15, Circular E, *Employer's Tax Guide.* Both are available at www.irs.gov.

If you fail to follow the IRS requirements for an accountable plan, the money you reimburse or advance will be subject to income tax withholding, and payment of Social Security and Medicare taxes.

RESOURCE

For more on employee reimbursement, see *Deduct It! Lower Your Small Business Taxes,* by Stephen Fishman (Nolo).

Wage and Hour Record keeping Requirements

The Fair Labor Standards Act requires you to keep detailed records for every employee who isn't exempt from that law. The explanations in Chapter 3 will help you determine whether your employee is or is not exempt. Here is the information you must keep in your records:

- employee's name, address, Social Security number, gender, occupation—and, if the employee is younger than 19, his or her age
- time and day when employee's workweek begins
- hours worked each day and total hours worked each workweek

- basis on which employee's wages are paid
- regular hourly pay rate
- total daily or weekly straight-time earnings
- total overtime earnings for the workweek
- all additions to or deductions from the employee's wages
- total wages paid each pay period, and
- date of payment and the pay period covered by the payment.

You can use any timekeeping method you choose. For example, you can use a time clock, keep track of the work hours yourself, or have your employee write down his or her time. Assuming you have a conscientious employee, the last method will usually be the best. The only requirement is that timekeeping must be complete and accurate. Here is one possible format:

Sample Time Record

Employee name _____

Week of _____

	Morning		Afternoon		Evening		Daily hours worked
	Time In	Time Out	Time In	Time Out	Time In	Time Out	
Sunday							
Monday							
Tuesday							
Wednesday							
Thursday							
Friday							
Saturday							

Total workweek hours in the pay period _____

Your employee may be on a fixed schedule from which he or she rarely deviates. In that case, you can keep a record showing the normal schedule of daily and weekly hours, and just indicate that your employee followed the schedule. When your employee works more or fewer hours, you can record the exceptions from the normal workweek.

 CAUTION

Record keeping requirements differ for some exempt employees. In particular, there are stricter requirements for employees who are exempt from the minimum wage or overtime pay provisions. For details, go to the U.S. Department of Labor website at www.dol.gov. To learn of any additional records your state may require you to keep, contact your state's labor department. You'll find state contact information at www.dol.gov/esa/contacts/state_of.htm.

Keep your wages and hour records for at least three years. You'll need them if the government or your employee questions whether you've met your pay obligations. You'll also need to keep records of employment taxes. (See Chapter 11 for a detailed explanation of this.) ●

Handling Payroll and Other Taxes

Chapter 10 described the payroll taxes that you must calculate and then deduct from your employee's paychecks. This chapter covers how you submit payroll taxes to the IRS, including the employer's share of Social Security and Medicare taxes. It also explains the federal tax forms you must file during the year and at year's end, and finally, describes what related records the IRS requires you to keep for reference.

Payroll Taxes Defined

Payroll taxes include:

- the income tax you must withhold from your employee's paycheck
- the Social Security and Medicare taxes you withhold, and
- your share of Social Security and Medicare taxes—an amount equal to what you withhold from your employee's paycheck for those taxes.

Computing Payroll Taxes

The total amount for Social Security and Medicare taxes should equal 15.3% of your employee's gross earnings.

That percentage consists of four components:

The employee's share of Social Security tax	6.2%
The employee's share of Medicare tax	1.45%
The employer's share of Social Security tax	6.2%
The employer's share of Medicare tax	<u>1.45%</u>
Total	15.3%

After your employee has earned $102,000, there is no further Social Security tax for the rest of the year, but the Medicare tax continues. It is unlikely, in most small businesses, that a first employee's earnings will exceed this cap.

⊘ **CAUTION**

The payroll tax figures can change. For updates, check the latest edition of IRS Publication 15, *Circular E, Employer's Tax Guide.* Once your business has obtained an Employer Identification Number, the IRS will periodically send you *Circular E.* If you haven't received this circular yet, go to www.irs.gov where you can view it or download it.

Depositing Payroll Taxes

Most small employers must deposit payroll taxes either monthly or quarterly throughout the year, and file IRS Form 941, *Employer's Quarterly Federal Tax Return*, each quarter. These deposits consist of your share and your employee's share of Social Security and Medicare taxes— the 15.3% described above—and the income tax you've withheld from your employee's paychecks.

The IRS may notify an employer whose annual payroll taxes will be likely be $1,000 or less to use IRS Form 944, *Employer's Annual Federal Tax Return*, instead; if your business receives such a notice, follow the special rules for depositing payroll taxes. (See "Employers Filing Annual Returns—Form 944," below.)

💡 **TIP**

If you don't get the forms in the mail. The IRS will periodically send you Form 941 or 944 preprinted with your business name, address, and Employer Identification Number. If you have not received the preprinted version by the time you must complete and file it, you can go to www.irs.gov and print out the form and instructions.

How to Deposit

If you make monthly or quarterly deposits, you can do so either through a bank or electronically. Both methods are described below.

Depositing Through a Bank

You can deposit the taxes at most banks, which will send them on to the U.S. Treasury. With each payment, you'll need to give the teller a Federal Tax Deposit (FTD) coupon—IRS Form 8109-B. When you obtain an Employer Identification Number, or EIN, the IRS will send you a coupon book preprinted with your business's name, address, and EIN. If you don't receive your coupon book promptly, call 800-829-4933 and request it.

In making your deposit, carefully darken the correct ovals on the coupon to indicate the tax period and type of tax. "Type of tax" means the IRS form your business uses to report employment taxes: Form 941 for those reporting quarterly or Form 944 for those reporting annually. Darken the 941 oval unless the IRS has informed you that your business is to file annually, in which case you'll darken the 944 oval.

> **TIP**
> **Ask the teller for a receipt.** Having a receipt can be a lifesaver if the bank or the IRS makes a mistake and you need to produce proof of a deposit.

Depositing Electronically

If your computer is linked to your bank account, you can deposit your taxes electronically. The government charges no fee for this service, but your bank may impose a service charge. Many banks will waive this fee, however, as part of the special services they provide to small business owners.

> **RESOURCE**
> To learn more about this method, go to www.eftps.gov and download IRS Publication 966, *Electronic Federal Tax Payment System Overview Brochure for Businesses and Individuals.*

When to Deposit

Your timetable for depositing payroll taxes will depend on the type of payroll tax return your business files. Most businesses must file a return quarterly using Form 941. A few—those that have been instructed to do so by the IRS—must file a return annually, using Form 944.

Employers Filing Quarterly Returns

If the IRS has not notified you to use Form 944, you will most likely need to deposit payroll taxes monthly. In that case, the deadline is the 15th day of the next month; for example, your deadline for depositing January payroll taxes is February 15. At the end of each quarter, you will file Form 941.

If your payroll taxes are less than $2,500 for a quarter, you may pay them quarterly instead of monthly. In that case, rather than depositing the taxes, you can simply send the funds to the IRS along with your quarterly Form 941 return.

The deadline for filing a quarterly return is the last day of the month following the quarter; for example, the deadline for filing the first quarterly return—covering January, February, and March—is April 30.

Payroll Tax Deposit Requirements for Form 941 Filers	
If your payroll tax liability is:	**You must deposit payroll taxes:**
$2,500 or more for a quarter	Monthly, by the 15th day of the next month
Less than $2,500 for a quarter	Either by the 15th day following the quarter, or with your quarterly return

Form 941 summarizes your payroll activity for a quarter of the year. If you haven't deposited enough payroll tax, enclose a check with Form 941 for any balance due.

The government uses the term "quarter" as follows:

First quarter: January, February, and March

Second quarter: April, May, and June

Third quarter: July, August, and September

Fourth quarter: October, November, and December

After you've filed your first Form 941, you need to file one every quarter, even though you may not have had any payroll tax liability for a given quarter.

TIP

Seasonal employers don't need to file quarterly. Typically, you're a seasonal employer if your employee works for you no more than four or five months a year. Let's say your business is a falafel stand that operates only from Memorial Day to Labor Day, or you rent out cross-country skis each winter at a Michigan resort. You can check the "Seasonal employer" box on line 17 of Form 941. The IRS will send you two 941s once a year after March 31. When completing the forms, check the box at the top that corresponds to the quarter reported.

Employers Filing Annual Returns

The IRS will notify you to use Form 944, *Employer's Annual Federal Tax Return*, if it determines that your payroll tax liability for the year will likely be $1,000 or less. You're likely to pay $1,000 or less in payroll taxes if you pay $4,000 or less in wages during the year. In this case, you must report your payroll taxes annually instead of quarterly, and must also follow special requirements for depositing payroll taxes. This reduces paperwork for many small businesses, as well as for the IRS.

Don't use Form 944 unless the IRS tells you to use it. The IRS sends a notice to by mid-February to employers who are required to use Form 944. If you haven't received a notice but think you qualify for an annual return, call the IRS at 800-829-0115. As a new employer, you can indicate on line 14 of your application for an EIN that you're likely to have $1,000 or less in payroll taxes for the calendar year. (See Chapter 5 for more on applying for an EIN.)

If you've been instructed to use Form 944, continue to do so unless the IRS notifies you in writing that it has changed your filing status. Even if you believe that your payroll taxes will exceed $1,000 for the year, wait for word from the IRS before switching to the quarterly Form 941.

Payroll Tax Deposit Requirements for Form 944 Filers	
If your payroll tax liability is:	**You must deposit payroll taxes:**
Less than $2,500 for the year	No deposit is required; you may pay the payroll taxes with your Form 944 annual return. (If you're not sure that your payroll tax liability will be less than $2,500 for the year, deposit under the rules below.)
$2,500 or more for the year, but less than $2,500 for the quarter	By the last day of the month after the quarter; if your fourth quarter liability is less than $2,500, you may pay those payroll taxes with your Form 944.
$2,500 or more for the quarter	Monthly

CAUTION

Make payroll taxes a priority. Make sure you pay these payroll taxes ahead of any other business debts. The reason is simple: The IRS can determine that you, as the owner of a small business, are personally liable for any payroll taxes that haven't been turned over to the government. This includes the income tax that you withheld or should have withheld, and the employee's share of Social Security and Medicare taxes.

The IRS can hold you responsible for payroll taxes even if you've limited your personal liability by forming a corporation or LLC, or if you've used a bookkeeper or accountant to handle your payroll. And even if you go through bankruptcy, you won't rid yourself of this debt.

RESOURCE

For more on payroll taxes, see *Tax Savvy for Small Business*, by Frederick W. Daily (Nolo).

State Employment Taxes

Each state has its own rules for paying employment taxes and for filing forms associated with them. Your state revenue department can provide details. You may also have to make periodic payments into a state unemployment fund; these payments typically are tied to the size of your payroll.

RESOURCE

For contact information about state unemployment taxes, go to www.workforcesecurity.doleta.gov/unemploy/agencies.asp.

Year-End Tax Filings

In addition to the monthly or quarterly tax responsibilities you must fulfill, you must also comply with a number of IRS filings related to employee earnings and taxes, with deadlines typically in January and February of each new year. If you've followed the guidance offered so far in this chapter, preparing your year-end paperwork should be a relatively painless chore.

The annual tax filing tasks and deadlines are summarized below. If a deadline date falls on a Saturday, Sunday, or federal holiday, you have until the next business day to complete the required task.

By January 31

- File Form 941, *Employer's Quarterly Federal Tax Return*, for the final quarter of the past year. Or if the IRS has instructed you to do so, file Form 944, *Employer's Annual Federal Tax Return*, covering the entire past year. These forms deal with withheld income tax and Social Security and Medicare taxes. If you deposited all payroll taxes on time, you have ten additional calendar days to file either Form 941 or 944.

- Give your employee a completed Form W-2, *Wage and Tax Statement*. This form lists your employee's total earnings for the year, as well as all the payroll deductions you've made.

- File Form 940, *Employer's Annual Federal Unemployment (FUTA) Tax Return*. You need to file this form—and pay the FUTA tax—if you paid wages of $1,500 during any calendar quarter, or if your employee worked at least some part of a day in any of 20 or more different weeks during the year. This tax is based on the first $7,000 of an employee's annual compensation. Chances are, if you have just one employee, the most you'll pay for this tax is $56. Most states also require businesses to pay an unemployment tax—sometimes through periodic payments throughout the year. Your state's labor department can provide details. For contact information, go to www.dol.gov/esa/contacts/state_of.htm.

By February 15

- Get a new Form W-4, *Employee's Withholding Allowance Certificate*, if your employee claimed exemption from income tax withholding last year and hasn't already given you a new form.

By February 28—or in a leap year, February 29

- File Form W-3, *Transmittal of Wage and Tax Statements*, with the Social Security Administration. Include Copy A of your employee's Form W-2. This lets the government credit your employee for Social Security and Medicare tax contributions that he or she made during the year, and those that your business made.

TIP

Order Forms W-2 and W-3 early. Unlike most other year-end forms, you can't go to the IRS site and print out Form W-2 and W-3 for submission to the government. The official versions of these forms are scannable, but the versions you download and print from the IRS website are not. To order useable copies, go to www.irs.gov/businesses/page/0,,id=23108,00.html. At the website, there's an order form you can use to obtain the official version of Forms W-2 and W-3. Another way to obtain the forms is to call 800-829-3676. Some post offices and public libraries may also stock them.

TIP

Consider filing Forms W-2 and W-3 electronically. You can go to www.socialsecurity.gov/employer, and select "Electronically File Your W-2s." After you register, you can create and file a completed version of your employee's Form W-2 for the Social Security Administration, and then print copies of that form to file with state and local governments, to give to your employee, and for your records. The system will also create Form W-3 based on the Form W-2 information. Filing these forms electronically can be a convenience if you have no fear of Internet glitches. Many small business owners still prefer to use paper forms and the U.S. mail for this annual chore.

During December

- Remind your employee to complete a new Form W-4, *Employee's Withholding Allowance Certificate*, if his or her withholding allowances have changed or will change for the next year.

Form Filing Requirements for Independent Contractors

Chapter 1 explains which workers can safely be classified as independent contractors rather than employees. During the year, you may have had one or more independent contractors do some work for your business—and if so, you may have year-end filing duties for them.

By January 31 of the new year, you must complete and give IRS Form 1099 MISC, *Miscellaneous Income*, to each independent contractor who received $600 or more from your business during the past year. Then, by February 28 or—in a leap year—by February 29, you must send a copy of each Form 1099 MISC to the IRS along with Form 1096, *Annual Summary and Transmittal of U.S. Information Returns.*

If you're going to need these forms, order them at www.irs.gov/businesses/page/0,,id=23108,00.html, or by calling 800-829-3676. As with Forms W-2 and W-3, the online versions of these forms cannot be printed and filed.

Unlike the payments you make to your employee, you're not expected to withhold income tax for payments to an independent contractor or to deduct or pay any Social Security or Medicare taxes.

CAUTION

You may also be required to file local and state year-end returns. Check with your state's revenue department to see what employment-related filings may be required. For contact information on state revenue departments, go to www.taxsites.com/agencies.html. To find other state-specific resources, go to www.sba.gov/localresources/index.html and click on the map. You'll be linked to the site for your state, where you can then pursue links to small business tax information.

Payroll Tax Record Keeping

The IRS requires you to keep records concerning payroll taxes because it may want to check up on those taxes someday. Your records should include:

- your EIN
- amounts and dates of wages
- tips reported by your employee
- your employee's name, address, Social Security number, and occupation
- dates of employment
- your employee's W-4 forms
- dates and amounts of electronic tax deposits
- copies of payroll tax returns, and
- records of fringe benefits and expense reimbursements, including supporting data.

You need to retain these records for at least four years. It's unlikely that the IRS will ever ask to see them, but it's best to play it safe. (See Chapter 8 for details on maintaining employee files.)

Deducting Employment Expenses

Many expenses related to having an employee are tax-deductible. Obviously, this is a good thing for you, because the more deductions your business has, the less income tax you or your business will have to pay. You deduct employment expenses from the business's gross income, reducing the bottom line on which taxes are computed. This chapter alerts you to the employment expenses you can deduct.

Deductible employment expenses are generally the same, regardless of whether your business is organized as a sole proprietorship, partnership, corporation, or limited liability company (LLC). However, the different business entities do use different IRS tax forms, and there are also differences in whether the business entity or its owners are directly responsible for the income tax bill. To help you sort this out, this chapter begins with a summary of how income gets taxed for various business forms, and where employee expense deductions are taken. It then describes various possible deductible expenses.

Reporting Income and Paying Taxes

Below is a summary of how each type of business entity reports its annual profit or loss to the IRS and who is responsible for paying federal income tax.

> **SKIP AHEAD**
>
> If you've been in business a while and have already filed income tax returns, you are probably familiar with the mechanics of the federal tax reporting system. You may wish to skim or skip this section, and go to "Deductible Employment Expenses," below.

Sole Proprietorships

As a sole proprietor, you report the profit—or the loss—from your business on Schedule C, *Profit or Loss From Business*, which is part of your personal Form 1040. Employment expense deductions are reported on Schedule C. The profit you report there is added to other income you may receive—and a loss is deducted from your other income. Your business does not file a separate federal tax return or pay any federal income tax.

Partnerships

Your partnership files IRS Form 1065, *U.S. Return of Partnership Income*, an informational return that tells the IRS how much the business earned or lost. The partnership deducts its employment expenses when computing its profit or loss.

As a partner, you get a Schedule K-1, *Partner's Share of Income, Credits, Deductions*, from the partnership notifying you of your share of profit or loss. You report your share on Schedule E, *Supplemental Income and Loss*, which is part of your Form 1040. Then you add your Schedule E income to your other income, or subtract any loss.

You pay income tax based on your net income from all sources. Your partnership does not pay any federal income tax.

Corporations

The federal tax procedures depend on whether you have a C corporation or an S corporation. You have a C corporation if you have not sent Form 2553, *Election by a Small Business Corporation*, to the IRS.

- **C Corporations.** Your corporation reports its profit or loss on either Form 1120 or 1120-A, U.S. Corporation Income Tax Return. The corporation deducts its employment expenses when computing profit or loss. If the corporation made a profit, it pays income tax on that profit. If the corporation paid you wages or dividends during the year, you report that income on your personal Form 1040 and pay income tax based on your net income from all sources.

- **S Corporations.** Your corporation files Form 1120-S, U.S. Income Tax Return for an S Corporation, notifying the IRS of the business's profit or loss. The corporation deducts its employment expenses when computing profit or loss. As a shareholder, you receive a Schedule K-1 from the corporation listing your share of profit or loss. You meld this number into your other 1040 figures and pay tax on your bottom line. Your corporation pays no federal income tax.

Single-Member LLCs

Your business doesn't file a federal income tax return or pay federal income tax. You deduct your LLC's employment expenses on Schedule C of your personal Form 1040, and report your LLC's profit or loss as if you were a sole proprietor. The profit or loss reported on your Schedule C is added to—or deducted from—your other income, and you pay tax on your net taxable income.

After consulting with a tax professional, you might decide that you'd like to have your LLC taxed as a C corporation. This might be a good choice, for example, if you want to leave some LLC income in the business coffers to finance its growth. In that case, you stand to pay less tax overall by electing to be taxed as a C corporation because, for the first $50,000 of taxable business income, the corporate tax rate and taxes paid will generally be lower than what you'd pay as an individual.

Although this sounds appealing, after paying yourself a reasonable wage, your business probably won't have much income to retain. For that reason, very few LLC owners choose the corporate tax option. If you're one of the exceptions, you must file IRS Form 8832, *Entity Classification Election.* Then your LLC will pay income tax on its profits, and you'll include the wages and distributions you received from the LLC on your 1040 and pay income tax based on your net income for the year.

Multimember LLCs

Your multimember LLC is treated as a partnership for federal income tax purposes. Your LLC sends the IRS a Form 1065, *U.S. Return of Partnership Income*—an informational return listing the LLC's profit or loss. The company gives you a Schedule K-1 indicating your share. The LLC deducts its employment expenses when computing its profit or loss.

You report your share on Schedule E of your 1040, and your profit or loss is then added to or subtracted from your income from other sources. You pay income tax based on your personal bottom line. Your LLC pays no federal income tax.

As explained just above, it is possible but highly unlikely that you and the other members of your LLC will elect to be taxed as a corporation. But if you do, you must file IRS Form 8832, *Entity Classification Election*. Then you'll follow the C corporation tax procedures summarized above. Your LLC will pay income tax on its profits, and you'll include your LLC wages and distributions on your 1040, paying income tax based on your net income for the year.

RESOURCE
For more information on taxation of differing business forms, see *Legal Guide for Starting and Running a Small Business,* by Fred S. Steingold (Nolo) and *Tax Savvy for Small Business,* by Frederick W. Daily (Nolo).

Deductible Expenses

Under federal tax laws, you can deduct a wide array of expenses related to being an employer, some of them more obvious than others. This section summarizes the main deductions that you should know about once you've hired your first employee.

Employee Pay

You can deduct the money you pay to your employee for his or her services. In most cases, this will be the gross amount of your employee's paychecks for the year. But the amount you can deduct for employee pay may include more than just wages or salary: It can also include bonuses and commissions, vacation pay, and sick pay that isn't covered by insurance.

Reimbursements for Business Expenses

You may periodically reimburse your employee for business-related expenses—such as airfare, lodging, meals, and entertainment—related to attending a trade show or industry convention, or expenses your employee incurs in dealing with clients, customers, or suppliers.

In some cases, you might advance money to your employee to cover such costs. In either case, you can deduct these expenses, although there are some limitations. For example, you can deduct only 50% of any business-related meal and entertainment expenses, even if you reimburse your employee 100% of the amount originally spent.

The IRS is particularly picky about these reimbursements and advances, so it is essential that you account for them. To qualify for deducting these reimbursements and advances, make sure your employee accounts for them within a reasonable time after they are incurred by giving you receipts, and by promptly returning any excess payment. (See Chapter 10 for details.)

Payroll Taxes

As explained in Chapters 10 and 11, as an employer, you must pay certain payroll taxes, including the:

• employer's share of Social Security tax

• employer's share of Medicare tax

• federal unemployment tax, and

• state payroll taxes, such as a state unemployment tax.

These payroll taxes are all deductible as employment expenses.

In deducting payroll taxes, do not include the amounts you've deducted from your employee's paychecks for income tax withholding or the *employee's* share of Social Security and Medicare taxes. Those amounts are included in your deduction for your employee's wages. Deduct your employee's gross earnings and the employer's share of Social Security and Medicare taxes.

EXAMPLE: Jose earns $18,000 working for Sonia's greeting card business. After Sonia withholds income tax and Jose's share of Social Security and Medicare taxes, Jose receives paychecks totaling $14,500. Sonia also pays $1,377 as the employer's share of Social Security and Medicare taxes. Sonia deducts the full $18,000 of Jose's wages and the $1,377 paid as the employer's share of Social Security and Medicare taxes.

Workers' Compensation Insurance

As explained in Chapter 9, most small businesses are required to buy workers' compensation insurance. This insurance pays wage and medical benefits if your employee is injured at work or suffers a work-related illness.

Depending on where your business is located, you may buy this coverage from a private insurance company or from a state agency. Either way, you can deduct the cost as an employment expense.

Education and Training Costs

You can deduct expenses for training your employee, such as the amount you spend for an educational seminar related to the business. As with all business expenses, to be deductible, the money you spend to train your employee must be both ordinary and necessary. An "ordinary" expense is defined as one that is common and accepted in your industry. A "necessary" expense is one that is helpful and appropriate for your trade or business. It doesn't have to be indispensable to be considered necessary.

EXAMPLE: Suzette hires Otto as an assistant in her real estate appraisal business. While Otto knows how to use word processing software and to navigate the Internet, he knows nothing about spreadsheet software, which is an important element of Suzette's business. Suzette sends Otto to a four-hour class that trains him to prepare and use spreadsheets, and she pays the $130 tuition fee. Sonia can deduct the fee.

RESOURCE

You can pay for certain educational expenses as part of an educational assistance program. For details, see IRS Publication 15-B, *Employer's Tax Guide to Fringe Benefits*. You can obtain it online at www.irs.gov.

Association Dues and Subscriptions

If you pay for your employee's membership in a trade association or for subscriptions to business publications, you can deduct the cost of them, too.

> **EXAMPLE:** Chen has a portrait studio. He hires another photographer, Alicia, to work for him. He pays Alicia's dues for membership in the Mid-America Photographic Society, and for her subscriptions to *Portrait Professional Monthly* and *Studio Economics*. Chen can deduct these expenses.

Equipment and Furniture

You can deduct the cost of equipment and furniture that you buy for your employee to use while conducting business for you. This might include, for example: a desk, chair, lamp, and computer.

Ordinarily, you're supposed to depreciate the cost of equipment and furniture by writing it off through tax deductions taken over a number of years. This is known as depreciation.

Here are the depreciation periods for some common types of business property:

Computer software	3 years
Computers and other office equipment	5 years
Cars and trucks	5 years
Desks, file cabinet, and safes	7 years

There's another way that small business owners can deduct the cost of equipment and furniture—and it allows you to write off the entire cost during the year in which you first use it. This option is called a Section 179 deduction, and is adjusted annually for inflation. In 2008, you can use Section 179 to immediately deduct up to $128,000. The cap will go down to $25,000 in 2010 unless Congress acts to increase it, which is likely because of the popularity of this option in the business community. As long as the Section 179 option remains available, you shouldn't need to fiddle around with depreciation schedules and the burdensome record keeping they entail.

RESOURCE

For in-depth information on depreciation, see IRS Publication 946, *How to Depreciate Property.* It is available online at www.irs.gov.

Inexpensive Gifts and Benefits

The IRS allows you to deduct certain low-cost benefits that you occasionally provide to your employee. The official term for the expenses that the IRS lets fly below its radar is "de minimis" benefits. The term covers property or services that have so little value that it would be impractical to account for them.

Examples include:

- occasional cocktail parties, company meals, or picnics for employees and guests
- traditional birthday or holiday gifts of property, other than cash, with a low fair-market value—for example, a turkey at Thanksgiving
- occasional theater or sporting event tickets
- coffee, doughnuts, and soft drinks
- flowers, fruit, books, or similar property you provide to your employee under special circumstances—for example, because of illness, outstanding performance, or family crisis, and
- occasional meals, meal money, or local transportation to enable your employee to work overtime—for example, ordering a pizza to be eaten at work or paying for a taxi ride home.

You cannot deduct cash or cash equivalent benefits, such as use of a gift card, charge card, or credit card, except for occasional meal money or transportation fare.

When a benefit qualifies as a deductible low-cost expense, your employee doesn't have to include it as part of his or her taxable income.

Other Fringe Benefits

The tax laws allow your business to deduct fringe benefits. But few of these fringes are likely to be viable for you if your business has just recently hired its first employee. As time goes on, however, you may want to offer a wider range of benefits to your employee—and to any future employees you hire.

The fringe benefits that the IRS considers deductible include:

- accident and health benefits
- achievement awards
- adoption assistance
- athletic facilities
- dependent care assistance
- educational assistance
- employee stock options
- group-term life insurance
- health savings accounts
- lodging on your business premises
- meals
- moving expense reimbursements
- retirement planning services
- transportation or commuting benefits
- tuition reduction, and
- working condition benefits, such as an employee's use of a company car for business or job-related education.

All of these items are governed by specific rules. If you follow the IRS rules, your business can deduct the cost of providing these benefits, and they won't be generally included in your employee's taxable income.

RESOURCE

To learn more, see IRS Publication 15-B, *Employer's Tax Guide to Fringe Benefits*, available online at www.irs.gov.

TIP

Owners can also receive fringe benefits. Your business can deduct the cost of many fringe benefits that it provides to you as an owner. For a detailed explanation of this, see *Tax Savvy for Small Business*, by Frederick W. Daily (Nolo).

Deducting Expenses for Bookkeeping and Tax Preparation

Hiring your first employee will add modestly to your record keeping, bookkeeping, and tax preparation burdens.

But with a bit of effort, you can learn all you need to know about these duties. And with the help of computer software such as *QuickBooks* or *QuickPay*, you can crunch the numbers, write your employee's paychecks, and complete all the required tax forms. The cost of such software is tax deductible, as is instruction in how to use it.

But for any number of reasons, you may prefer to farm out all or part of this work. You may, for example, sign on with a payroll service, or retain a bookkeeper or accountant to relieve you from the payroll and tax compliance chores. If you decide to hire such outside help, your business can deduct the amounts it pays for it.

RESOURCE

The following publications will help you deduct as much as possible for employment expenses:

- *Deduct It: Lower Your Small Business Taxes*, by Stephen Fishman (Nolo)
- *Tax Savvy for Small Business*, by Frederick W. Daily (Nolo)
- IRS Publication 15-B, *Employer's Tax Guide to Fringe Benefits*
- IRS Publication 334, *Tax Guide for Small Business*
- IRS Publication 463, *Travel, Entertainment, Gift and Car Expenses*
- IRS Publication 535, *Business Expenses*, and
- IRS Publication 946, *How to Depreciate Property*.

All the IRS publications are available at the agency's website: www.irs.gov.

Motivating Your Employee

Like every other employer, you'd like your employee to be loyal and hardworking—to give his or her very best effort day after day. When you made the decision to hire, you saw the possibilities: the many ways the employee could help your business grow and perhaps enable you to use your own time more efficiently.

How you treat your employee can greatly influence whether her or she will do just the minimum necessary to receive a paycheck, or will put heart and soul into the job.

This chapter introduces you to some of the ways you can motivate your employee, with special attention to filling needs that cannot be met by money alone.

Moving Beyond Money

Paying a decent salary and giving generous raises can help meet your employee's material needs. But money isn't everything—and in the working world, it's only a small part of the picture. Some of the intangible benefits mentioned in Chapter 4, such as good working conditions and flexible hours, can help motivate your employee to put forth more than the minimum time and effort.

But whether your employee will go the extra mile to help make your business a success usually depends on how effective you are in meeting individual emotional needs. Everyone has a need to be recognized and appreciated, a desire to feel that his or her work has meaning, and a wish to be treated with dignity and respect. Many people also strive to improve themselves—to learn and do more and experience personal growth. If you can tap into these basic emotional needs and help satisfy them, your employee is likely to put more energy and thought into the job.

Expressing Appreciation

Your employee needs to know that his or her work is noticed and appreciated. By taking notice of those efforts and praising an especially well done job, you'll reinforce outstanding performance—and the employee is likely to repeat and build on the traits you want to encourage. The beautiful thing is that you recognize and reward your employee's good work at little or no cost.

Something as simple as thanking an employee for a job well done can help motivate peak performance—and may even help unearth ways to refine and expand current work duties.

A number of examples of successful employer encouragement follow.

- "Joe, nice going in serving that last customer. You gave her great service, and I could see that she was very pleased. Are you interested in stepping up your hours in the front of the store?"

- "Ginny, that menu board you wrote up looks terrific. You have a nice, artistic touch. Would you like to revamp our printed menus, too?"

- "Tan, you're really getting the knack of trimming those boards to size. I think you're ready to learn the drill press now."

You can also motivate your employee and add dividends by recognizing your employee publicly, when a customer or client is present.

Here are some examples of such accolades in a public place:

- "Ron deserves all the credit for putting together that party tray. He makes everything look so appetizing, doesn't he?"

- "Keisha pulled together that estimate in no time flat. She's really quite a whiz."

- Or when Cindy comes by at noon to take her husband John to lunch, you might say: "John hit a home run this morning. He created an ad that knocked the socks off our client. I'm so glad he's part of Mackenzie Publicity."

TIP

Putting it on paper. You can also recognize your employee by featuring him or her in an ad in the local newspaper, with phrasing such as: "Meet Miguel Hernandez, our expert in installing network systems." A photo and some information about your employee's work may help motivate greater achievements on the job. But use caution. If your efforts seem insincere or condescending, your ad can be a turn-off to your employee. Before you use this technique, run the ad by a few trusted advisers. Better to run nothing than to publish an ad that may backfire.

Giving Small Gifts

You can recognize and reward excellent performance with a small or inexpensive gift such as flowers, a houseplant, or a basket of fruit— delivered along with a handwritten note of appreciation.

And you might also consider having the gift delivered to the employee's home. That way, the employee will gain enhanced esteem in the eyes of a spouse, partner, children, or other family members. Your employee can proudly display your gift and bask in the admiration of others. And the gift will convey a clear message: "You do good work and are valued outside of the house as well as at home."

Small gifts can also be personalized. If your employee is a jazz fan, a John Coltrane CD might be suitable reward—again with a personal note of thanks. For a sports fan, a set of tickets to a baseball or football game might do the trick. Or for a gourmand, a gift certificate for dinner for two at a fine restaurant. Here again the employee's achievement can be celebrated with a friend or a loved one. Also, consider a gift for the employee's child—again, a way for the employee to spread the good cheer.

After your employee has worked hard to complete a project or has dealt with an especially stressful situation, you might give him or her a day or two off—with pay.

As explained in Chapter 12, you can deduct small gifts as business expenses, and they're not included as part of your employee's income.

Encouraging Input

Ask your employee for suggestions about improving working conditions. If the answer is better lighting, a newer computer, or a chance to work at home one day a week, you can fairly easily accommodate the request— and likely help improve morale in the bargain.

Communicating Clearly

Be clear with your employee about what you expect. Spend time showing him or her the ropes, as your employee may not intuit how you want the job done.

And bear in mind that good communication goes both ways. Listen to your employee's comments and suggestions. Listening by itself demonstrates recognition and respect. And don't be surprised if your employee comes up with some ideas you can put to use. This could pay off, because if you receive the ideas and suggestions gracefully, your employee will likely be encouraged to offer more of them.

But when your employee isn't meeting expectations, communicate clearly how the performance is subpar, and help your employee rise to your standards. Chances are your employee wants to succeed and will do anything to avoid being labeled a bad worker. (See "Troubleshooting Problems," below.)

Allowing Room to Grow

Many employees value the chance to expand their skills and take on more responsibility. You can take the time to teach your employee yourself, or send him or her to a workshop or seminar for additional specific job training. Back at work, your employee will be motivated to try new skills—and your business will reap the benefits.

Most employees also value autonomy—that is, being entrusted with tasks they can carry out on their own, without close supervision. Your employee is sure to be motivated and strive to do well if you delegate responsible work to him or her.

Assure your employee that nothing bad will happen if he or she makes a mistake—and then honor that promise. Everyone who makes decisions will make mistakes now and then, and everyone learns from them. Your employee is likely to be motivated and want to earn the trust that you've placed in him or her. Of course, you must use discretion in delegating. You don't want to create a sink-or-swim situation in which one mistake spells disaster for the employee or your business.

Showing Dignity and Respect

To motivate your employee to excel, treat him or her with dignity and respect at all times.

As discussed in more detail below, you can and should point out any aspects of the employee's work that need improvement, but always put that criticism in terms of the job and not the person. Personal criticism or insults will always be a turnoff, and will likely cause the employee to become resentful or angry.

 TIP

Maintain and insist on high standards of integrity. Values matter. Employees are likely to become demoralized if their employers cut corners, or cheat or lie—or pretend not to see unethical behavior by employees. By contrast, employees generally feel pride in working for an employer who observes high ethical standards. Make it clear by your example that your business operates honestly and above-board at all times, and that you expect similar behavior from your employee—even if it sometimes means less profit for the business.

Troubleshooting Problems

Doing periodic performance evaluations can give your employee a chance to improve if performance is substandard. Performance reviews can keep small problems from growing into big ones. And if you later need to fire your employee, it won't come as a surprise if he or she had some earlier warning about subpar performance.

By putting your evaluations in writing and saving them in your employee's file, you have a credible history of documented problems you can use if you later need to defend a termination, for example. The evaluations will help establish that you treated your employee fairly.

It is a good idea to formally evaluate your employee twice a year—and more often if there are problems on the job. For consistency, you can develop a form that focuses on how well your employee has performed job duties—and you can use the same form for each evaluation.

Complete the form before you meet with your employee, following these guidelines.

- Give a balanced picture of the employee's strengths and weaknesses.
- Use specific examples of how the employee has met, exceeded, or fallen short of expectations.
- Let your employee know the areas that need improvement. Set objective goals to meet.
- If your employee's performance is substantially below par, set a date to meet again to review progress.
- Clearly inform your employee when a failure to improve may lead to being fired.

Leave space on the form for your employee to comment on the evaluation and to acknowledge receiving a copy of it.

Once you've completed the written evaluation, meet with your employee in private to go over it. It's usually a good idea to begin and end the meeting on a positive note, sandwiching negative material in between. Remember, too, that your employee will likely find it easier to accept criticism—and try to improve behavior—if you focus on workplace performance, not on individual personality.

Whatever your approach, tell it like it is. Should you later have legal trouble because you fired your employee, a judge or jury won't look at your evaluations in a vacuum. For example, they'll sense that something is wrong if you consistently rate your employee's performance as poor or mediocre, but continue to hand out generous raises or entrust him or her with greater and greater responsibilities. The logical conclusion: You didn't take seriously the criticisms in your evaluation report, so you shouldn't have expected your employee to take them seriously, either.

Just as damaging is to give your employee glowing praise in report after report—perhaps to make him or her feel good—and then wield the ax for a single infraction. That smacks of unfairness—and unfair employers often lose court fights, especially in situations where a sympathetic employee appears to have been treated harshly.

TIP

Once is not enough. Giving feedback about workplace competence and expectations should be an ongoing process. The written evaluation should be a culmination of the oral feedback you've been informally giving your employee. Your goal is to have no surprises about how your employee is doing. Keep the employee informed of any problems so that the two of you can work together to correct them.

You can also ask your employee to evaluate how *you* are doing. You'll benefit by making the evaluation process a two-way street. Listen carefully to what your employee says. You're likely to learn a thing or two.

RESOURCE

For an in-depth discussion of employee evaluations, including step-by-step instructions and sample forms, see *The Performance Appraisal Handbook: Legal & Practical Rules for Managers*, by Amy DelPo.

Sample Employee Evaluation Form

The form below can be adapted to meet your personal style and the type of work your employee performs for your business.

CONFIDENTIAL
Employee Performance Evaluation

Employee name _____

Job title _____

Reviewer _____

Review date _____

JOB PERFORMANCE
(In responding, give specific examples of strengths and weaknesses as often as possible.)

General Quality of Work
(Focus on accuracy, attention to detail, originality, timeliness, organization, degree of supervision needed to accomplish tasks.)

_____

_____

Dependability
(Focus on attendance, punctuality, attentiveness, ability to follow instructions, ability to meet deadlines.)

_____

_____

Job Knowledge
(Focus on level of knowledge and skills required to master work, willingness to take the initiative in tackling new tasks.)

_____

_____

_____

Personality

(Focus on cooperativeness, decision-making skills, ability to work for and with others, ability to handle confrontations.)

_____

_____

Communication Skills

(Focus on ability to use language effectively, ability to express ideas clearly and grammatically, command of oral and written language, ability to explain concepts to others.)

_____

_____

Management Ability

(Focus on ability to identify problems, ability to creatively solve problems, ability to plan, assign, and schedule workload, ability to guide an individual or group to complete a task.)

_____

_____

Other Job Requirements

(Focus on specific needs of your business or needs for individual improvement: public contact, self-development, quality control, ability to stay within cost guidelines.)

PERFORMANCE SUMMARY

What are the employee's outstanding and strongest points?

_____

_____

_____

What are the employee's shortcomings and weaknesses?

_____

_____

Specific accomplishments and changes since last performance review.

_____

_____

GOALS FOR IMPROVEMENT

What can the employee do to be more effective or make needed improvements?

_____

_____

_____

What additional training or equipment would be helpful?

_____

In what ways could the job be changed to make better use of the employee's skills and abilities?

_____

EMPLOYEE FEEDBACK

(To be completed by the employee.)

What are your most important accomplishments on the job so far?

_____

_____

What are your weakest job performance areas or those most in need of improvement?

_____

_____

What steps could you take to improve?

_____

_____

What can management do to support your efforts to improve?

_____

_____

Other work concerns you would like to discuss.

_____

_____

NEXT REVIEW

Date scheduled for next review _____

Particular areas targeted for improvement:

_____

_____

_____

Employee signature: _____

Date: _____

Reviewer's signature _____

Date: _____

Index

Get the Latest in the Law

 Nolo's Legal Updater
We'll send you an email whenever a new edition of your book is published!
Sign up at **www.nolo.com/legalupdater**.

 Updates at Nolo.com
Check **www.nolo.com/update** to find recent changes in the law that
affect the current edition of your book.

 Nolo Customer Service
To make sure that this edition of the book is the most recent one, call us at
800-728-3555 and ask one of our friendly customer service representatives
(7:00 am to 6:00 pm PST, weekdays only). Or find out at **www.nolo.com**.

Complete the Registration & Comment Card ...
... and we'll do the work for you! Just indicate your preferences below:

Registration & Comment Card

NAME _____ DATE _____

ADDRESS _____

CITY _____ STATE _____ ZIP _____

PHONE _____ EMAIL _____

COMMENTS _____

WAS THIS BOOK EASY TO USE?   (VERY EASY)   5   4   3   2   1   (VERY DIFFICULT)

☐ Yes, you can quote me in future Nolo promotional materials. *Please include phone number above.*

☐ Yes, send me **Nolo's Legal Updater** via email when a new edition of this book is available.

Yes, I want to sign up for the following email newsletters:

   ☐ **NoloBriefs** (monthly)
   ☐ **Nolo's Special Offer** (monthly)
   ☐ **Nolo's BizBriefs** (monthly)
   ☐ **Every Landlord's Quarterly** (four times a year)

☐ Yes, you can give my contact info to carefully selected
partners whose products may be of interest to me.

HEMP1

Send to: **Nolo** 950 Parker Street Berkeley, CA 94710-9867, Fax: (800) 645-0895, or include all of
the above information in an email to regcard@nolo.com with the subject line "HEMP1."

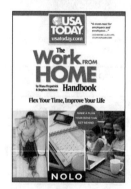
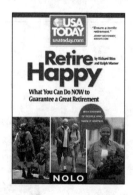

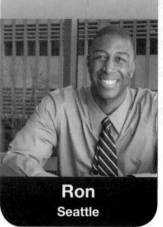